# 50 Heritage and Grain Recipes for Home

By: Kelly Johnson

# Table of Contents

- Quinoa-stuffed bell peppers
- Spicy lentil curry
- Traditional Irish soda bread
- Greek-style barley salad
- Moroccan couscous tagine
- Italian farro risotto with mushrooms
- Mexican black bean and corn salad
- Ethiopian injera flatbread
- Indian spiced rice pilaf
- Chinese fried rice with vegetables
- Japanese sushi rolls
- Egyptian koshari
- Russian buckwheat blini with smoked salmon
- Swedish rye bread with pickled herring
- Nigerian jollof rice
- Peruvian quinoa soup
- Lebanese tabbouleh salad
- Brazilian black bean stew
- Spanish paella
- Thai green curry with jasmine rice
- Armenian bulgur pilaf
- Scottish oatcakes
- South African mealie pap
- Jamaican rice and peas
- Turkish bulgur köfte (meatballs)
- Korean bibimbap
- French ratatouille with quinoa
- Vietnamese spring rolls with rice vermicelli
- Hawaiian poi
- Israeli couscous salad
- German spaetzle with cheese sauce
- Bangladeshi khichuri
- Venezuelan arepas
- Finnish rye bread with smoked salmon
- Cuban moros y cristianos (black beans and rice)

- Thai mango sticky rice
- Afghan rice pilaf with raisins and carrots
- Polish pierogi with buckwheat filling
- Canadian maple syrup oatmeal
- Belgian waffles with berries
- Dutch poffertjes (mini pancakes)
- Malaysian nasi lemak
- Georgian khachapuri (cheese bread)
- Filipino arroz caldo (rice porridge)
- Sri Lankan coconut roti
- Tunisian couscous with lamb
- Hungarian goulash with barley
- Czech potato dumplings with sauerkraut
- Norwegian lefse (potato flatbread)
- Brazilian tapioca crepes with coconut filling

**Quinoa-stuffed bell peppers**

Ingredients:

- 4 large bell peppers (any color)
- 1 cup quinoa, rinsed
- 2 cups vegetable broth or water
- 1 tablespoon olive oil
- 1 small onion, diced
- 2 cloves garlic, minced
- 1 can (14 oz) black beans, drained and rinsed
- 1 cup corn kernels (fresh, frozen, or canned)
- 1 teaspoon ground cumin
- 1 teaspoon chili powder
- Salt and pepper to taste
- 1 cup shredded cheese (cheddar, Monterey Jack, or your favorite cheese)
- Fresh cilantro or parsley for garnish (optional)

Instructions:

1. Preheat your oven to 375°F (190°C). Lightly grease a baking dish large enough to hold the bell peppers upright.
2. Cut the tops off the bell peppers and remove the seeds and membranes from the inside. Place the peppers upright in the prepared baking dish and set aside.
3. In a medium saucepan, combine the quinoa and vegetable broth or water. Bring to a boil, then reduce the heat to low, cover, and simmer for about 15-20 minutes, or until the quinoa is cooked and the liquid is absorbed. Remove from heat and set aside.
4. In a large skillet, heat the olive oil over medium heat. Add the diced onion and cook until softened, about 3-4 minutes. Add the minced garlic and cook for an additional 1 minute, until fragrant.
5. Add the cooked quinoa, black beans, corn, ground cumin, chili powder, salt, and pepper to the skillet with the onions and garlic. Stir well to combine and cook for another 2-3 minutes to heat everything through.
6. Spoon the quinoa mixture into the prepared bell peppers, pressing down gently to pack the filling tightly. Top each pepper with shredded cheese.

7. Cover the baking dish with foil and bake in the preheated oven for 25-30 minutes, or until the peppers are tender and the cheese is melted and bubbly.
8. Remove the foil and bake for an additional 5 minutes to lightly brown the cheese, if desired.
9. Once done, remove the stuffed peppers from the oven and let them cool for a few minutes before serving. Garnish with fresh cilantro or parsley, if desired.
10. Serve the quinoa-stuffed bell peppers hot, optionally with a side of salsa, guacamole, or sour cream. Enjoy your nutritious and flavorful meal!

**Spicy lentil curry**

Ingredients:

- 1 cup dried lentils (brown or green), rinsed and drained
- 2 tablespoons olive oil
- 1 onion, finely chopped
- 3 cloves garlic, minced
- 1 tablespoon fresh ginger, grated
- 1 teaspoon ground turmeric
- 1 teaspoon ground cumin
- 1 teaspoon ground coriander
- 1/2 teaspoon cayenne pepper (adjust to taste)
- 1 can (14 oz) diced tomatoes
- 1 can (14 oz) coconut milk
- 1 cup vegetable broth or water
- Salt and pepper to taste
- Fresh cilantro, chopped, for garnish
- Cooked rice or naan bread, for serving

Instructions:

1. Heat the olive oil in a large pot or Dutch oven over medium heat. Add the chopped onion and cook until softened, about 5 minutes.
2. Add the minced garlic and grated ginger to the pot, and cook for another 1-2 minutes until fragrant.
3. Stir in the ground turmeric, ground cumin, ground coriander, and cayenne pepper, and cook for another minute to toast the spices.
4. Add the rinsed lentils to the pot, along with the diced tomatoes (with their juices), coconut milk, and vegetable broth or water. Stir to combine.
5. Bring the mixture to a simmer, then reduce the heat to low and cover the pot with a lid. Let the curry simmer gently for about 20-25 minutes, stirring occasionally, or until the lentils are tender and the curry has thickened.
6. Taste and adjust the seasoning with salt and pepper as needed.
7. If the curry is too thick, you can add more vegetable broth or water to reach your desired consistency.
8. Once the lentils are cooked to your liking, remove the pot from the heat.

9. Serve the spicy lentil curry hot, garnished with chopped fresh cilantro. Serve with cooked rice or warm naan bread on the side.
10. Enjoy your delicious and comforting lentil curry as a satisfying vegetarian main dish!

**Traditional Irish soda bread**

Ingredients:

- 4 cups all-purpose flour
- 1 teaspoon baking soda
- 1 teaspoon salt
- 1 and 3/4 cups buttermilk (or substitute with 1 and 3/4 cups milk mixed with 1 and 3/4 tablespoons lemon juice or white vinegar, let sit for 5 minutes before using)

Instructions:

1. Preheat your oven to 425°F (220°C). Lightly grease a baking sheet or line it with parchment paper.
2. In a large mixing bowl, whisk together the all-purpose flour, baking soda, and salt until well combined.
3. Make a well in the center of the flour mixture and pour in the buttermilk.
4. Using a wooden spoon or your hands, gently mix the buttermilk into the flour mixture until a dough forms. Be careful not to overmix; the dough should be soft and slightly sticky.
5. Turn the dough out onto a lightly floured surface and gently knead it for about 1 minute, just until it comes together into a smooth ball. Shape the dough into a round loaf.
6. Place the loaf onto the prepared baking sheet. Use a sharp knife to score a deep cross into the top of the loaf, about 1/2 inch deep. This helps the bread to bake evenly.
7. Bake the Irish soda bread in the preheated oven for 15 minutes. Then reduce the oven temperature to 400°F (200°C) and continue to bake for another 25-30 minutes, or until the bread is golden brown and sounds hollow when tapped on the bottom.
8. Transfer the baked bread to a wire rack and let it cool completely before slicing.
9. Serve slices of traditional Irish soda bread with butter and your favorite jam or spread. Enjoy it warm or at room temperature as a delightful accompaniment to soups, stews, or as a snack.

10. Store any leftovers in an airtight container at room temperature for up to 2 days, or freeze for longer storage. Reheat slices in a toaster or oven before serving, if desired.

Enjoy the rustic simplicity and hearty flavor of this traditional Irish soda bread!

**Greek-style barley salad**

Ingredients:

- 1 cup barley, rinsed
- 2 and 1/2 cups water or vegetable broth
- 1 cucumber, diced
- 1 pint cherry tomatoes, halved
- 1/2 red onion, finely chopped
- 1/2 cup Kalamata olives, pitted and sliced
- 1/2 cup crumbled feta cheese
- 1/4 cup chopped fresh parsley
- 1/4 cup chopped fresh mint
- 1/4 cup extra virgin olive oil
- 2 tablespoons lemon juice
- 1 garlic clove, minced
- Salt and pepper to taste

Instructions:

1. In a medium saucepan, combine the barley and water or vegetable broth. Bring to a boil over high heat, then reduce the heat to low, cover, and simmer for about 30-35 minutes, or until the barley is tender and the liquid is absorbed. Remove from heat and let it cool.
2. In a large mixing bowl, combine the cooked barley, diced cucumber, halved cherry tomatoes, chopped red onion, sliced Kalamata olives, crumbled feta cheese, chopped parsley, and chopped mint.
3. In a small bowl, whisk together the extra virgin olive oil, lemon juice, minced garlic, salt, and pepper to make the dressing.
4. Pour the dressing over the barley salad and toss gently to coat all the ingredients evenly.
5. Taste and adjust the seasoning with more salt and pepper, if needed.
6. Cover the bowl with plastic wrap and refrigerate the barley salad for at least 1 hour to allow the flavors to meld together.
7. Before serving, give the salad a final toss and adjust the seasoning, if necessary.
8. Serve the Greek-style barley salad chilled or at room temperature as a side dish or light meal. Enjoy its vibrant flavors and wholesome goodness!

9. Store any leftovers in an airtight container in the refrigerator for up to 2-3 days. The flavors may intensify as the salad sits, making it even more delicious the next day.

This Greek-style barley salad is perfect for picnics, potlucks, or as a healthy lunch option. It's packed with fiber, vitamins, and minerals, making it both nutritious and delicious!

**Moroccan couscous tagine**

Ingredients:

- 1 cup couscous
- 1 and 1/2 cups vegetable broth or water
- 2 tablespoons olive oil
- 1 onion, finely chopped
- 2 cloves garlic, minced
- 1 teaspoon ground cumin
- 1 teaspoon ground coriander
- 1 teaspoon ground cinnamon
- 1/2 teaspoon ground turmeric
- 1/2 teaspoon paprika
- Pinch of saffron threads (optional)
- 1 can (14 oz) chickpeas, drained and rinsed
- 1 cup diced carrots
- 1 cup diced zucchini
- 1 cup diced eggplant
- 1 cup diced tomatoes
- 1/4 cup chopped dried apricots
- 1/4 cup chopped dried figs
- 1/4 cup chopped fresh cilantro or parsley, for garnish
- Salt and pepper to taste
- Lemon wedges, for serving

Instructions:

1. In a medium saucepan, bring the vegetable broth or water to a boil. Stir in the couscous, cover the saucepan, and remove it from the heat. Let the couscous steam for about 5 minutes, then fluff it with a fork to separate the grains. Set aside.
2. In a large tagine or Dutch oven, heat the olive oil over medium heat. Add the chopped onion and cook until softened, about 5 minutes.
3. Add the minced garlic, ground cumin, ground coriander, ground cinnamon, ground turmeric, paprika, and saffron threads (if using) to the tagine. Cook for another minute until the spices are fragrant.

4. Add the drained chickpeas, diced carrots, diced zucchini, diced eggplant, and diced tomatoes to the tagine. Stir well to combine.
5. Cover the tagine and let the vegetables cook for about 10-15 minutes, or until they are tender but still slightly firm.
6. Once the vegetables are cooked, stir in the chopped dried apricots and chopped dried figs. Cook for another 2-3 minutes to heat through.
7. Taste the vegetable mixture and adjust the seasoning with salt and pepper, if needed.
8. To serve, spoon the cooked couscous onto a serving platter or individual plates. Top with the vegetable mixture from the tagine.
9. Garnish the Moroccan couscous tagine with chopped fresh cilantro or parsley.
10. Serve hot, with lemon wedges on the side for squeezing over the dish. Enjoy the aromatic flavors of this Moroccan-inspired meal!

This Moroccan couscous tagine is a hearty and satisfying dish that's perfect for sharing with family and friends. It's packed with vegetables, chickpeas, and fragrant spices, making it a flavorful and nutritious meal option.

**Italian farro risotto with mushrooms**

Ingredients:

- 1 cup farro
- 4 cups vegetable broth
- 2 tablespoons olive oil
- 1 onion, finely chopped
- 2 cloves garlic, minced
- 8 oz mushrooms (such as cremini or shiitake), sliced
- 1/2 cup dry white wine
- 1/2 cup grated Parmesan cheese
- Salt and pepper to taste
- Fresh parsley, chopped, for garnish

Instructions:

1. In a medium saucepan, bring the vegetable broth to a simmer over medium heat. Reduce the heat to low to keep it warm.
2. In a separate large saucepan or skillet, heat the olive oil over medium heat. Add the chopped onion and cook until softened, about 5 minutes.
3. Add the minced garlic to the pan and cook for another 1-2 minutes until fragrant.
4. Add the sliced mushrooms to the pan and cook, stirring occasionally, until they are tender and browned, about 5-7 minutes.
5. Stir in the farro and cook for another 2-3 minutes, allowing the grains to toast slightly.
6. Pour in the dry white wine and cook, stirring constantly, until the wine has been absorbed by the farro.
7. Begin adding the warm vegetable broth to the farro mixture, one ladleful at a time, stirring frequently. Allow each addition of broth to be absorbed before adding more. Continue this process until the farro is tender and has a creamy consistency, similar to traditional risotto. This will take about 30-40 minutes.
8. Once the farro is cooked to your liking, stir in the grated Parmesan cheese until it is melted and incorporated into the risotto.
9. Taste the risotto and season with salt and pepper to taste.
10. Serve the Italian farro risotto with mushrooms hot, garnished with freshly chopped parsley.

11. Enjoy the rich and flavorful combination of farro and mushrooms in this Italian-inspired dish!

**Mexican black bean and corn salad**

Ingredients:

- 1 can (15 oz) black beans, drained and rinsed
- 1 cup corn kernels (fresh, frozen, or canned)
- 1 red bell pepper, diced
- 1/2 red onion, finely chopped
- 1 jalapeño pepper, seeded and finely chopped (optional)
- 1/4 cup chopped fresh cilantro
- Juice of 2 limes
- 2 tablespoons olive oil
- 1 teaspoon ground cumin
- 1/2 teaspoon chili powder
- Salt and pepper to taste
- Avocado slices, for garnish (optional)

Instructions:

1. In a large mixing bowl, combine the black beans, corn kernels, diced red bell pepper, finely chopped red onion, chopped jalapeño pepper (if using), and chopped fresh cilantro.
2. In a small bowl, whisk together the lime juice, olive oil, ground cumin, chili powder, salt, and pepper to make the dressing.
3. Pour the dressing over the black bean and corn mixture in the large bowl. Toss gently to coat all the ingredients evenly with the dressing.
4. Taste the salad and adjust the seasoning with more salt and pepper, if needed.
5. Cover the bowl with plastic wrap and refrigerate the black bean and corn salad for at least 30 minutes to allow the flavors to meld together.
6. Before serving, give the salad a final toss to redistribute the dressing.
7. Garnish the Mexican black bean and corn salad with avocado slices, if desired.
8. Serve the salad chilled as a side dish or light meal. Enjoy its fresh and zesty flavors!

This Mexican black bean and corn salad is packed with protein, fiber, and nutrients, making it both delicious and nutritious. It's perfect for potlucks, picnics, barbecues, or as a quick and easy meal option any day of the week.

**Ethiopian injera flatbread**

Ingredients:

- 2 cups teff flour (you can also use a blend of teff and all-purpose flour)
- 3 cups water
- 1/2 teaspoon salt
- Vegetable oil or clarified butter (niter kibbeh), for greasing the pan

Instructions:

1. In a large mixing bowl, combine the teff flour and water. Stir until well combined and smooth. Cover the bowl with a clean kitchen towel and let the mixture ferment at room temperature for at least 24 to 48 hours. This fermentation process gives injera its characteristic tangy flavor.
2. After the fermentation period, you'll notice that the mixture has risen and developed bubbles on the surface.
3. Stir the batter gently and add the salt, mixing until fully incorporated.
4. Heat a non-stick skillet or injera pan over medium heat. Lightly grease the pan with vegetable oil or clarified butter.
5. Pour a ladleful of the injera batter onto the hot pan, swirling it around to spread it into a thin, even layer. The injera should be about 1/4 inch thick.
6. Cover the pan with a lid and cook the injera for 1-2 minutes, or until bubbles form on the surface and the edges begin to lift from the pan.
7. Unlike traditional pancakes, injera is only cooked on one side. You'll know it's done when the surface is dry and no longer shiny.
8. Using a spatula, carefully remove the injera from the pan and transfer it to a plate or platter. Repeat the process with the remaining batter, greasing the pan as needed.
9. Stack the cooked injera on top of each other as you go, covering them with a clean kitchen towel to keep them warm and prevent them from drying out.
10. Serve the injera flatbread alongside your favorite Ethiopian dishes, such as wots (stews), tibs (sautéed meats), or vegetables. Tear off pieces of injera and use them to scoop up the savory dishes.
11. Enjoy the authentic taste and texture of homemade Ethiopian injera flatbread with your meal!

Note: If you don't have teff flour, you can use a blend of teff and all-purpose flour. Traditional injera is made with 100% teff flour, but using a blend can yield similar results while being more accessible. Adjust the ratio to your preference.

**Indian spiced rice pilaf**

Ingredients:

- 1 cup basmati rice
- 2 cups water
- 2 tablespoons ghee or vegetable oil
- 1 small onion, finely chopped
- 2 cloves garlic, minced
- 1-inch piece of ginger, grated
- 1 cinnamon stick
- 2 green cardamom pods
- 4 whole cloves
- 1 bay leaf
- 1/2 teaspoon cumin seeds
- 1/2 teaspoon ground turmeric
- 1/2 teaspoon ground coriander
- 1/4 teaspoon ground cayenne pepper (adjust to taste)
- Salt to taste
- 1/4 cup chopped mixed nuts (such as almonds, cashews, and pistachios)
- 1/4 cup golden raisins or dried cranberries
- Fresh cilantro, chopped, for garnish (optional)

Instructions:

1. Rinse the basmati rice under cold water until the water runs clear. Drain well and set aside.
2. In a medium saucepan, heat the ghee or vegetable oil over medium heat. Add the chopped onion and cook until softened and translucent, about 5 minutes.
3. Add the minced garlic and grated ginger to the saucepan, and cook for another 1-2 minutes until fragrant.
4. Add the cinnamon stick, green cardamom pods, whole cloves, bay leaf, and cumin seeds to the saucepan. Cook, stirring constantly, for about 1 minute to toast the spices.
5. Stir in the ground turmeric, ground coriander, ground cayenne pepper, and salt to taste. Cook for another minute to bloom the spices.

6. Add the rinsed basmati rice to the saucepan and stir to coat the grains with the spiced onion mixture.
7. Pour in the water and bring the mixture to a boil over high heat. Once boiling, reduce the heat to low, cover the saucepan with a tight-fitting lid, and simmer for about 15-20 minutes, or until the rice is tender and the liquid is absorbed. Avoid stirring the rice while it cooks to prevent it from becoming mushy.
8. While the rice is cooking, heat a small skillet over medium heat. Add the chopped mixed nuts and toast them, stirring frequently, until lightly golden and fragrant, about 3-4 minutes. Remove from heat and set aside.
9. Once the rice is cooked, fluff it with a fork to separate the grains. Gently stir in the toasted nuts and golden raisins or dried cranberries.
10. Transfer the Indian spiced rice pilaf to a serving platter or bowl. Garnish with fresh chopped cilantro, if desired.
11. Serve the pilaf hot as a flavorful side dish or as a main course. Enjoy the aromatic spices and rich flavors of this delicious Indian-inspired dish!

Note: You can customize this recipe by adding other ingredients such as vegetables (like peas, carrots, or bell peppers) or protein (such as cooked chicken, shrimp, or tofu) to make it a complete meal. Adjust the spices and seasoning according to your taste preferences.

**Chinese fried rice with vegetables**

Ingredients:

- 2 cups cooked rice (preferably day-old, such as jasmine or long-grain)
- 2 tablespoons vegetable oil or sesame oil
- 2 cloves garlic, minced
- 1-inch piece of ginger, grated
- 1 small onion, finely chopped
- 1 carrot, diced
- 1 bell pepper (any color), diced
- 1 cup frozen peas or mixed vegetables, thawed
- 2 eggs, lightly beaten
- 2 tablespoons soy sauce
- 1 tablespoon oyster sauce (optional)
- Salt and pepper to taste
- 2 green onions, chopped, for garnish
- Toasted sesame seeds, for garnish (optional)

Instructions:

1. Heat a large skillet or wok over medium-high heat. Add 1 tablespoon of vegetable oil or sesame oil to the skillet.
2. Add the minced garlic and grated ginger to the skillet, and cook for about 30 seconds until fragrant.
3. Add the chopped onion to the skillet and cook until softened and translucent, about 2-3 minutes.
4. Push the cooked onion to one side of the skillet, then add another tablespoon of oil to the empty side. Pour the beaten eggs into the skillet and scramble them until they are fully cooked.
5. Once the eggs are cooked, add the diced carrot and bell pepper to the skillet. Stir-fry for about 3-4 minutes until the vegetables are tender but still slightly crisp.
6. Add the cooked rice to the skillet, breaking up any clumps with a spatula. Stir-fry the rice with the vegetables for another 2-3 minutes until heated through.
7. Stir in the thawed peas or mixed vegetables, and cook for another minute to warm them up.

8. Drizzle the soy sauce and oyster sauce (if using) over the rice mixture, and toss everything together until well combined. Season with salt and pepper to taste.
9. Continue to cook the fried rice for another 2-3 minutes, stirring constantly, until everything is heated through and evenly coated with the sauce.
10. Remove the skillet from the heat and transfer the Chinese fried rice to a serving platter or bowl.
11. Garnish the fried rice with chopped green onions and toasted sesame seeds, if desired.
12. Serve the Chinese fried rice with vegetables hot as a delicious and satisfying main course or side dish. Enjoy the savory flavors and vibrant colors of this classic Chinese dish!

Note: Feel free to customize this recipe by adding other ingredients such as cooked chicken, shrimp, tofu, or additional vegetables like broccoli or mushrooms. Adjust the seasoning and sauce according to your taste preferences.

**Japanese sushi rolls**

Ingredients:

- 2 cups sushi rice
- 2 cups water
- 3 tablespoons rice vinegar
- 2 tablespoons sugar
- 1 teaspoon salt
- Nori seaweed sheets
- Fillings of your choice (such as cucumber, avocado, crab meat, smoked salmon, tuna, or cooked shrimp)
- Soy sauce, for serving
- Pickled ginger, for serving
- Wasabi, for serving

Instructions:

1. Rinse the sushi rice under cold water until the water runs clear. Drain well.
2. In a medium saucepan, combine the rinsed sushi rice and water. Bring to a boil over high heat, then reduce the heat to low, cover, and simmer for about 15-20 minutes, or until the rice is cooked and the water is absorbed.
3. While the rice is cooking, in a small saucepan, combine the rice vinegar, sugar, and salt. Heat over low heat until the sugar and salt are dissolved. Remove from heat and let it cool.
4. Once the rice is cooked, transfer it to a large mixing bowl. Gradually add the seasoned rice vinegar to the rice, folding it in gently with a spatula or rice paddle to combine. Be careful not to overmix or mash the rice. Allow the seasoned rice to cool to room temperature.
5. Prepare your fillings by slicing them into thin strips or pieces. You can use a variety of ingredients such as cucumber, avocado, crab meat, smoked salmon, tuna, or cooked shrimp.
6. Place a bamboo sushi rolling mat (makisu) on a clean work surface. Lay a sheet of nori seaweed on the mat, shiny side down.
7. With wet hands, spread a thin layer of seasoned sushi rice evenly over the nori seaweed, leaving a 1-inch border along the top edge.

8. Arrange your desired fillings in a row across the center of the rice-covered nori seaweed.
9. Starting from the bottom edge closest to you, lift the bamboo sushi rolling mat and roll it up tightly, using your fingers to tuck in the fillings as you roll. Apply gentle pressure to shape the sushi roll.
10. Once the sushi roll is tightly rolled, use a sharp knife to slice it into individual pieces. Wipe the knife clean with a damp cloth between cuts to ensure clean slices.
11. Repeat the process with the remaining nori seaweed sheets, rice, and fillings until all the ingredients are used.
12. Serve the sushi rolls with soy sauce, pickled ginger, and wasabi on the side for dipping.
13. Enjoy your homemade Japanese sushi rolls as a delicious and satisfying meal or snack!

Note: Feel free to get creative with your sushi roll fillings and combinations. You can also experiment with different sauces and toppings to customize your rolls to your taste preferences. Have fun and enjoy the process of making and eating sushi!

**Egyptian koshari**

Ingredients:

For the Koshari:

- 1 cup dried brown lentils
- 1 cup long-grain white rice
- 1 cup elbow macaroni or ditalini pasta
- 2 tablespoons vegetable oil
- Salt to taste

For the Tomato Sauce:

- 2 tablespoons vegetable oil
- 1 onion, finely chopped
- 3 cloves garlic, minced
- 1 can (14 oz) diced tomatoes
- 2 tablespoons tomato paste
- 1 teaspoon ground cumin
- 1 teaspoon ground coriander
- 1/2 teaspoon cayenne pepper (optional)
- Salt and pepper to taste

For the Fried Onions:

- 1 large onion, thinly sliced
- Vegetable oil for frying

For Serving:

- Chickpeas (canned or cooked from dried)
- Dukkah (optional)
- Chopped fresh cilantro or parsley (optional)

Instructions:

1. Rinse the lentils under cold water and pick out any debris. Place them in a large saucepan and cover with water. Bring to a boil, then reduce the heat to low and simmer for about 20-25 minutes, or until the lentils are tender but not mushy. Drain and set aside.
2. In a separate saucepan, cook the rice according to package instructions. Fluff with a fork and set aside.
3. Cook the pasta according to package instructions until al dente. Drain and set aside.
4. To make the tomato sauce, heat the vegetable oil in a saucepan over medium heat. Add the chopped onion and cook until softened and translucent, about 5 minutes. Add the minced garlic and cook for another minute until fragrant.
5. Stir in the diced tomatoes, tomato paste, ground cumin, ground coriander, and cayenne pepper (if using). Season with salt and pepper to taste. Simmer the sauce for about 15-20 minutes, stirring occasionally, until it thickens slightly.
6. While the sauce is simmering, prepare the fried onions. Heat vegetable oil in a large skillet over medium-high heat. Add the thinly sliced onions and fry until golden brown and crispy, about 8-10 minutes. Remove with a slotted spoon and drain on paper towels.
7. To assemble the koshari, layer the cooked lentils, rice, and pasta in a serving dish. Top with a generous amount of the tomato sauce and sprinkle with the crispy fried onions.
8. Serve the koshari hot, garnished with chickpeas, a sprinkle of dukkah (if using), and chopped fresh cilantro or parsley, if desired.
9. Enjoy this hearty and flavorful Egyptian koshari as a delicious and satisfying meal!

Note: Koshari is often served with a spicy garlic vinegar sauce called "dakka" on the side. Feel free to drizzle some over the koshari for extra flavor.

**Russian buckwheat blini with smoked salmon**

Ingredients:

For the Buckwheat Blini:

- 1 cup buckwheat flour
- 1 cup all-purpose flour
- 1 teaspoon baking powder
- 1/2 teaspoon salt
- 2 large eggs
- 1 and 1/2 cups milk
- 2 tablespoons melted butter, plus more for cooking
- Vegetable oil for greasing

For Serving:

- Smoked salmon slices
- Sour cream or crème fraîche
- Fresh dill, chopped
- Lemon wedges

Instructions:

1. In a large mixing bowl, whisk together the buckwheat flour, all-purpose flour, baking powder, and salt until well combined.
2. In a separate bowl, beat the eggs lightly, then whisk in the milk and melted butter until smooth.
3. Gradually add the wet ingredients to the dry ingredients, whisking until you have a smooth batter. Let the batter rest for about 15-20 minutes to allow the flour to hydrate.
4. Heat a non-stick skillet or griddle over medium heat. Lightly grease the skillet with butter or oil.

5. Pour about 1/4 cup of batter onto the skillet for each blini, spreading it out slightly with the back of a spoon to form a small circle. Cook for 1-2 minutes, or until bubbles start to form on the surface and the edges begin to set.
6. Flip the blini and cook for another 1-2 minutes on the other side, until golden brown and cooked through. Transfer the cooked blini to a plate and cover with a clean kitchen towel to keep warm.
7. Repeat the process with the remaining batter, greasing the skillet as needed, until all the blini are cooked.
8. To serve, top each buckwheat blini with a slice of smoked salmon. Add a dollop of sour cream or crème fraîche on top of the salmon.
9. Garnish with chopped fresh dill and serve with lemon wedges on the side.
10. Enjoy the Russian buckwheat blini with smoked salmon as a delicious appetizer or elegant brunch dish!

Note: You can also serve the buckwheat blini with additional toppings such as caviar, chopped red onion, capers, or horseradish cream for a gourmet twist.

**Swedish rye bread with pickled herring**

Ingredients:

For the Rye Bread:

- 2 cups dark rye flour
- 1 cup whole wheat flour
- 1 cup all-purpose flour
- 2 teaspoons instant yeast
- 1 teaspoon salt
- 2 tablespoons honey or maple syrup
- 1 and 1/2 cups warm water
- 2 tablespoons vegetable oil
- 1 tablespoon caraway seeds (optional)

For Serving:

- Pickled herring fillets
- Red onion, thinly sliced
- Fresh dill, for garnish
- Sour cream or crème fraîche (optional)

Instructions:

1. In a large mixing bowl, combine the dark rye flour, whole wheat flour, all-purpose flour, instant yeast, salt, and caraway seeds (if using). Mix well to combine.
2. In a separate bowl, whisk together the warm water and honey or maple syrup until the sweetener is dissolved.
3. Make a well in the center of the dry ingredients and pour in the wet ingredients along with the vegetable oil.
4. Using a wooden spoon or your hands, mix the ingredients together until a rough dough forms.
5. Turn the dough out onto a lightly floured surface and knead for about 5-7 minutes, or until the dough is smooth and elastic.

6. Shape the dough into a ball and place it in a lightly greased bowl. Cover the bowl with a clean kitchen towel or plastic wrap and let the dough rise in a warm, draft-free place for about 1-1.5 hours, or until doubled in size.
7. Once the dough has risen, preheat your oven to 375°F (190°C). Punch down the dough to release any air bubbles, then shape it into a loaf and place it on a parchment-lined baking sheet.
8. Cover the loaf with a clean kitchen towel and let it rise for another 30-45 minutes, or until slightly puffed.
9. Using a sharp knife, score the top of the loaf with a few shallow slashes.
10. Bake the rye bread in the preheated oven for 30-35 minutes, or until the loaf is golden brown and sounds hollow when tapped on the bottom.
11. Remove the bread from the oven and let it cool completely on a wire rack before slicing.
12. To serve, slice the Swedish rye bread and top each slice with pickled herring fillets. Garnish with thinly sliced red onion and fresh dill.
13. Serve the Swedish rye bread with pickled herring as an appetizer or part of a traditional Swedish smörgåsbord. You can also add a dollop of sour cream or crème fraîche on top if desired.

Enjoy the delightful combination of flavors and textures in this classic Scandinavian dish!

**Nigerian jollof rice**

Ingredients:

- 2 cups long-grain parboiled rice
- 2 tablespoons vegetable oil or palm oil
- 1 onion, finely chopped
- 2-3 tomatoes, blended into a puree
- 1 red bell pepper, blended into a puree
- 1 green bell pepper, diced
- 1 scotch bonnet pepper (optional), finely chopped
- 2 cloves garlic, minced
- 1 teaspoon ground cayenne pepper (optional)
- 1 teaspoon ground paprika
- 1 teaspoon ground thyme
- 1 teaspoon ground curry powder
- 1 teaspoon ground ginger
- 2 cups chicken or vegetable broth
- Salt to taste
- Fresh cilantro or parsley, chopped, for garnish

Instructions:

1. Rinse the parboiled rice under cold water until the water runs clear. Drain well and set aside.
2. In a large skillet or pot, heat the vegetable oil over medium heat. Add the chopped onion and cook until softened and translucent, about 5 minutes.
3. Add the minced garlic and diced green bell pepper to the skillet. Cook for another 2-3 minutes until fragrant.
4. Stir in the blended tomato and red bell pepper puree. Cook the mixture, stirring occasionally, for about 10-15 minutes until the liquid reduces and thickens slightly.
5. Add the chopped scotch bonnet pepper (if using), ground cayenne pepper (if using), ground paprika, ground thyme, ground curry powder, and ground ginger to the skillet. Stir well to combine and cook for another 2-3 minutes to allow the spices to bloom.
6. Pour in the chicken or vegetable broth and bring the mixture to a simmer.

7. Stir in the parboiled rice, making sure it is evenly coated with the sauce. Season with salt to taste.
8. Cover the skillet or pot with a tight-fitting lid and reduce the heat to low. Let the rice simmer for about 20-25 minutes, or until the rice is cooked through and the liquid is absorbed.
9. Once the rice is cooked, fluff it with a fork to separate the grains.
10. Serve the Nigerian jollof rice hot, garnished with chopped fresh cilantro or parsley.

Enjoy the vibrant colors and rich flavors of this delicious Nigerian jollof rice! It's perfect as a main dish or served alongside your favorite protein and side dishes.

**Peruvian quinoa soup**

Ingredients:

- 1 cup quinoa, rinsed
- 1 tablespoon vegetable oil
- 1 onion, finely chopped
- 2 cloves garlic, minced
- 1 carrot, diced
- 1 bell pepper, diced
- 1 cup diced tomatoes (fresh or canned)
- 1 teaspoon ground cumin
- 1 teaspoon ground paprika
- 1/2 teaspoon dried oregano
- 6 cups vegetable or chicken broth
- Salt and pepper to taste
- Fresh cilantro or parsley, chopped, for garnish
- Lime wedges, for serving

Instructions:

1. Rinse the quinoa under cold water until the water runs clear. Drain well and set aside.
2. In a large pot or Dutch oven, heat the vegetable oil over medium heat. Add the chopped onion and cook until softened and translucent, about 5 minutes.
3. Add the minced garlic to the pot and cook for another minute until fragrant.
4. Stir in the diced carrot and bell pepper, and cook for 3-4 minutes until slightly softened.
5. Add the diced tomatoes, ground cumin, ground paprika, and dried oregano to the pot. Cook, stirring occasionally, for about 5 minutes to allow the flavors to meld together.
6. Pour in the vegetable or chicken broth and bring the mixture to a boil.
7. Once boiling, stir in the rinsed quinoa and reduce the heat to low. Cover the pot and let the soup simmer for about 15-20 minutes, or until the quinoa is cooked and tender.
8. Season the soup with salt and pepper to taste. Adjust the seasoning as needed.

9. Ladle the Peruvian quinoa soup into serving bowls and garnish with chopped fresh cilantro or parsley.
10. Serve the soup hot, with lime wedges on the side for squeezing over the soup just before eating.

Enjoy the comforting and nutritious flavors of this delicious Peruvian quinoa soup! It's perfect for warming up on chilly days and makes a satisfying meal on its own or served with crusty bread or a side salad.

## Lebanese tabbouleh salad

- 1/2 cup bulgur wheat
- 1 cup boiling water
- 2 cups finely chopped fresh parsley
- 1/2 cup finely chopped fresh mint leaves
- 2 medium tomatoes, diced
- 1 small red onion, finely chopped
- 1/4 cup freshly squeezed lemon juice
- 1/4 cup extra virgin olive oil
- Salt and pepper to taste
- Optional: 1/4 cup chopped green onions or scallions

Instructions:

1. Place the bulgur wheat in a heatproof bowl and pour the boiling water over it. Stir to combine, then cover the bowl with a lid or plastic wrap and let it sit for about 20-30 minutes, or until the bulgur is tender and has absorbed the water.
2. Fluff the cooked bulgur wheat with a fork and let it cool to room temperature.
3. In a large mixing bowl, combine the cooled bulgur wheat, finely chopped parsley, finely chopped mint leaves, diced tomatoes, and finely chopped red onion. If using, add the chopped green onions or scallions.
4. In a small bowl, whisk together the freshly squeezed lemon juice and extra virgin olive oil to make the dressing. Season with salt and pepper to taste.
5. Pour the dressing over the tabbouleh salad mixture and toss everything together until well combined and evenly coated with the dressing.
6. Taste the tabbouleh salad and adjust the seasoning with more salt, pepper, or lemon juice if needed.
7. Cover the bowl with plastic wrap and refrigerate the tabbouleh salad for at least 30 minutes to allow the flavors to meld together.
8. Before serving, give the tabbouleh salad a final toss and adjust the seasoning if necessary.
9. Serve the Lebanese tabbouleh salad chilled as a refreshing side dish or light meal. Enjoy its fresh and vibrant flavors!

This Lebanese tabbouleh salad is perfect for picnics, potlucks, or as a side dish to accompany grilled meats or fish. It's also a great option for a healthy and satisfying lunch.

**Brazilian black bean stew**

Ingredients:

- 2 cups dried black beans
- Water for soaking and cooking
- 2 tablespoons vegetable oil
- 1 onion, chopped
- 4 cloves garlic, minced
- 2 bay leaves
- 1 teaspoon ground cumin
- 1 teaspoon smoked paprika
- 1/2 teaspoon dried oregano
- Salt and pepper to taste
- 1 lb (450g) smoked sausage or linguica, sliced
- 1 lb (450g) pork shoulder or loin, cubed
- 1 lb (450g) pork ribs or bacon, chopped
- 1 orange, sliced (optional, for serving)
- Cooked white rice, for serving
- Chopped fresh cilantro, for garnish

Instructions:

1. Rinse the dried black beans under cold water and remove any debris. Place them in a large bowl and cover with water. Let them soak overnight, or for at least 8 hours.
2. Drain the soaked black beans and transfer them to a large pot. Cover the beans with fresh water and bring to a boil over high heat. Reduce the heat to low and simmer, partially covered, for about 1-1.5 hours, or until the beans are tender.
3. While the beans are cooking, heat the vegetable oil in a large skillet or Dutch oven over medium heat. Add the chopped onion and minced garlic, and sauté until softened and fragrant, about 5 minutes.
4. Stir in the bay leaves, ground cumin, smoked paprika, dried oregano, salt, and pepper. Cook for another minute to toast the spices.
5. Add the sliced smoked sausage or linguica to the skillet and cook until lightly browned, about 5 minutes.

6. Add the cubed pork shoulder or loin and chopped pork ribs or bacon to the skillet. Cook, stirring occasionally, until the meat is browned on all sides, about 8-10 minutes.
7. Transfer the cooked meat mixture to the pot with the cooked black beans. Stir everything together to combine.
8. Continue to simmer the Brazilian black bean stew, uncovered, for another 30-45 minutes, or until the flavors have melded together and the stew has thickened to your desired consistency.
9. Taste the stew and adjust the seasoning with more salt and pepper if needed.
10. Serve the Brazilian black bean stew hot, accompanied by slices of orange (if using) and cooked white rice. Garnish with chopped fresh cilantro.
11. Enjoy this hearty and flavorful Brazilian dish with your family and friends!

Note: Brazilian black bean stew is often served with traditional accompaniments such as farofa (toasted cassava flour), orange slices, and shredded kale. Feel free to customize the dish according to your taste preferences.

## Spanish paella

Ingredients:

- 1.5 cups paella rice (such as Bomba or Calasparra rice)
- 4 cups chicken or vegetable broth
- 1 pinch saffron threads
- 2 tablespoons olive oil
- 1 onion, finely chopped
- 4 cloves garlic, minced
- 1 red bell pepper, diced
- 1 yellow bell pepper, diced
- 1 tomato, diced
- 1 teaspoon smoked paprika
- Salt and pepper to taste
- 1 lb (450g) mixed seafood (such as shrimp, mussels, clams, and/or squid), cleaned and prepared
- 1/2 lb (225g) chicken or rabbit meat, diced (optional)
- 1/2 cup frozen peas
- Lemon wedges, for serving
- Fresh parsley, chopped, for garnish

Instructions:

1. In a small bowl, combine the saffron threads with a few tablespoons of warm water and let them steep for about 10-15 minutes to release their flavor and color.
2. In a large paella pan or skillet, heat the olive oil over medium heat. Add the diced onion and sauté until softened, about 5 minutes.
3. Add the minced garlic to the pan and cook for another minute until fragrant.
4. Stir in the diced red and yellow bell peppers, and cook for about 5 minutes until they begin to soften.
5. Add the diced tomato to the pan and cook for another 5 minutes until it breaks down and becomes saucy.
6. Sprinkle the smoked paprika over the vegetables and stir to combine. Season with salt and pepper to taste.
7. Add the paella rice to the pan and stir to coat it with the vegetable mixture.

8. Pour the saffron-infused water (along with the saffron threads) over the rice, followed by the chicken or vegetable broth. Stir gently to combine.
9. Bring the broth to a simmer, then reduce the heat to low and let the rice cook undisturbed for about 15-20 minutes, or until most of the liquid is absorbed and the rice is nearly cooked.
10. Arrange the mixed seafood (and diced chicken or rabbit, if using) evenly over the partially cooked rice. Scatter the frozen peas over the top.
11. Cover the paella pan with a lid or aluminum foil and continue to cook for another 10-15 minutes, or until the seafood is cooked through and the rice is tender.
12. Once the paella is cooked, remove it from the heat and let it rest, covered, for a few minutes before serving.
13. Garnish the Spanish paella with chopped fresh parsley and serve hot, with lemon wedges on the side for squeezing over the paella.
14. Enjoy this delicious and authentic Spanish dish with family and friends!

Note: Feel free to customize your paella with your favorite seafood, meats, and vegetables. Traditional paella pans have a wide and shallow shape, which helps to create a crispy layer of rice called "socarrat" at the bottom of the pan. If you don't have a paella pan, you can use a large skillet or wide, shallow pot instead.

**Thai green curry with jasmine rice**

Ingredients:

For the Green Curry Paste:

- 2-3 green Thai chilies, chopped (adjust to taste)
- 2 shallots, chopped
- 4 cloves garlic, chopped
- 1 stalk lemongrass, chopped (white part only)
- 1-inch piece of galangal or ginger, chopped
- 1 bunch fresh cilantro, stems and leaves separated
- 2 tablespoons chopped fresh basil leaves
- 1 tablespoon chopped fresh kaffir lime leaves (or use zest of 1 lime)
- 1 teaspoon ground coriander
- 1 teaspoon ground cumin
- 1/2 teaspoon ground white pepper
- 1/2 teaspoon shrimp paste (optional)
- 2 tablespoons vegetable oil

For the Curry:

- 1 tablespoon vegetable oil
- 2-3 tablespoons Thai green curry paste (homemade or store-bought)
- 1 can (14 oz) coconut milk
- 1 cup chicken or vegetable broth
- 2 tablespoons fish sauce (or soy sauce for a vegetarian version)
- 1 tablespoon palm sugar or brown sugar
- 1 small eggplant, diced
- 1 red bell pepper, sliced
- 1 cup sliced bamboo shoots (canned or fresh)
- 1 cup sliced mushrooms (such as button or shiitake)
- 1 lb (450g) protein of your choice (such as chicken, shrimp, tofu, or seitan), sliced or cubed
- Fresh Thai basil leaves, for garnish
- Fresh cilantro leaves, for garnish
- Cooked jasmine rice, for serving

Instructions:

1. To make the green curry paste, combine all the ingredients in a food processor or blender. Blend until smooth, adding a little water if needed to help the mixture blend. Set aside.
2. In a large skillet or pot, heat the vegetable oil over medium heat. Add 2-3 tablespoons of the green curry paste (adjust to taste) and cook for 1-2 minutes until fragrant.
3. Pour in the coconut milk and chicken or vegetable broth. Stir to combine and bring the mixture to a simmer.
4. Add the fish sauce (or soy sauce) and palm sugar (or brown sugar) to the curry. Stir until the sugar is dissolved.
5. Add the diced eggplant, sliced red bell pepper, bamboo shoots, and sliced mushrooms to the curry. Cook for 5-7 minutes until the vegetables are tender.
6. Add the sliced or cubed protein of your choice (chicken, shrimp, tofu, or seitan) to the curry. Cook for another 5-7 minutes until the protein is cooked through.
7. Taste the curry and adjust the seasoning with more fish sauce (or soy sauce) if needed.
8. Remove the curry from the heat and stir in the fresh Thai basil leaves.
9. Serve the Thai green curry hot, accompanied by cooked jasmine rice.
10. Garnish the curry with additional fresh cilantro leaves and Thai basil leaves, if desired.
11. Enjoy this fragrant and flavorful Thai green curry with jasmine rice!

Note: You can customize this recipe by adding other vegetables such as snow peas, baby corn, or zucchini. Adjust the spiciness of the curry by adding more or fewer green Thai chilies. You can also make the curry ahead of time and reheat it before serving for a quick and easy meal.

**Armenian bulgur pilaf**

Ingredients:

- 1 cup medium or coarse bulgur wheat
- 2 cups water or vegetable broth
- 2 tablespoons olive oil
- 1 onion, finely chopped
- 2 cloves garlic, minced
- 2 tomatoes, diced
- 1 tablespoon tomato paste
- 1 teaspoon paprika
- 1/2 teaspoon ground cumin
- Salt and pepper to taste
- Fresh parsley, chopped, for garnish
- Lemon wedges, for serving

Instructions:

1. Rinse the bulgur wheat under cold water until the water runs clear. Drain well and set aside.
2. In a large skillet or pot, heat the olive oil over medium heat. Add the chopped onion and sauté until softened and translucent, about 5 minutes.
3. Add the minced garlic to the skillet and cook for another minute until fragrant.
4. Stir in the diced tomatoes, tomato paste, paprika, ground cumin, salt, and pepper. Cook, stirring occasionally, for about 5-7 minutes until the tomatoes break down and become saucy.
5. Add the rinsed bulgur wheat to the skillet and stir to coat it with the tomato mixture.
6. Pour in the water or vegetable broth and bring the mixture to a simmer.
7. Once simmering, reduce the heat to low and cover the skillet with a lid. Let the bulgur pilaf cook for about 15-20 minutes, or until the bulgur is tender and has absorbed all the liquid.
8. Remove the skillet from the heat and let the bulgur pilaf rest, covered, for a few minutes.
9. Fluff the bulgur pilaf with a fork to separate the grains.

10. Serve the Armenian bulgur pilaf hot, garnished with chopped fresh parsley and accompanied by lemon wedges for squeezing over the pilaf.
11. Enjoy this flavorful and nutritious dish as a side dish or as a light meal on its own!

Note: You can customize this recipe by adding other ingredients such as diced bell peppers, carrots, or cooked chickpeas for extra flavor and texture. Adjust the seasoning according to your taste preferences.

**Scottish oatcakes**

Ingredients:

- 1 cup oatmeal (medium or fine)
- 1/2 cup all-purpose flour
- 1/2 teaspoon baking powder
- Pinch of salt
- 2 tablespoons butter, melted
- Approximately 1/4 cup hot water

Instructions:

1. Preheat your oven to 350°F (175°C) and lightly grease a baking sheet or line it with parchment paper.
2. In a mixing bowl, combine the oatmeal, all-purpose flour, baking powder, and salt.
3. Pour the melted butter over the dry ingredients and mix well to combine.
4. Gradually add hot water to the mixture, a little at a time, stirring until you have a stiff dough. You may not need to use all the water, so add it gradually until the dough comes together.
5. Roll out the dough on a lightly floured surface to about 1/4 inch thickness.
6. Using a round cookie cutter or the rim of a glass, cut out rounds of dough and place them on the prepared baking sheet.
7. Prick each oatcake with a fork to prevent them from puffing up too much while baking.
8. Bake in the preheated oven for about 20-25 minutes, or until the oatcakes are lightly golden brown and firm to the touch.
9. Remove from the oven and transfer the oatcakes to a wire rack to cool completely.
10. Once cooled, store the oatcakes in an airtight container at room temperature for up to a week.

Scottish oatcakes are delicious served plain or with a variety of toppings such as cheese, butter, jam, or smoked salmon. They're perfect for breakfast, as a snack, or as part of a cheese board. Enjoy!

**South African mealie pap**

Ingredients:

- 2 cups maize meal (white or yellow)
- 4 cups water
- Pinch of salt (optional)

Instructions:

1. In a large pot, bring the water to a boil over medium-high heat.
2. Once the water is boiling, gradually pour in the maize meal while stirring continuously to prevent lumps from forming.
3. Reduce the heat to low and continue to cook the maize meal, stirring frequently, for about 15-20 minutes or until it thickens and reaches the desired consistency. The pap should have a smooth texture and be thick enough to hold its shape.
4. If desired, season the pap with a pinch of salt to taste.
5. Once the pap is cooked, remove it from the heat and let it rest for a few minutes before serving.
6. Serve the South African mealie pap hot as a breakfast porridge with milk and sugar, or as a side dish with savory accompaniments such as tomato and onion gravy, stewed meats, or vegetables.
7. Leftover pap can be stored in the refrigerator for a few days. To reheat, simply add a little water or milk to loosen the pap and warm it up on the stovetop or in the microwave until heated through.

South African mealie pap is a comforting and versatile dish that can be enjoyed in many different ways. It's a staple food in South African cuisine and is often served at traditional gatherings, celebrations, and braais (barbecues).

## Jamaican rice and peas

Ingredients:

- 2 cups long-grain rice (such as jasmine or basmati)
- 1 can (15 oz) red kidney beans, drained and rinsed
- 1 can (13.5 oz) coconut milk
- 2 cups water or vegetable broth
- 1 onion, finely chopped
- 2 cloves garlic, minced
- 1-2 green onions, chopped
- 1 sprig fresh thyme (or 1 teaspoon dried thyme)
- 1 Scotch bonnet pepper (whole or sliced, optional)
- 1 teaspoon ground allspice
- Salt and pepper to taste

Instructions:

1. In a large pot or Dutch oven, combine the rice, kidney beans, coconut milk, water or vegetable broth, chopped onion, minced garlic, chopped green onions, fresh thyme, whole or sliced Scotch bonnet pepper (if using), ground allspice, salt, and pepper.
2. Stir to combine all the ingredients.
3. Place the pot over medium-high heat and bring the mixture to a boil.
4. Once boiling, reduce the heat to low, cover the pot with a tight-fitting lid, and let the rice and peas simmer for about 20-25 minutes, or until the rice is cooked and the liquid is absorbed. Avoid stirring the rice too much to prevent it from becoming mushy.
5. Once the rice is cooked, remove the pot from the heat and let it sit, covered, for a few minutes to allow the flavors to meld together.
6. Remove the Scotch bonnet pepper (if used) and the sprig of fresh thyme before serving.
7. Fluff the rice and peas with a fork and transfer them to a serving dish.
8. Serve the Jamaican rice and peas hot as a delicious side dish to accompany your favorite Jamaican main dishes.

Jamaican rice and peas is a comforting and aromatic dish with a rich and creamy texture from the coconut milk. It's packed with flavor and pairs perfectly with a variety of Jamaican dishes. Enjoy!

**Turkish bulgur köfte (meatballs)**

Ingredients:

For the bulgur mixture:

- 1 cup fine bulgur
- 1 cup hot water
- 1 onion, finely chopped
- 2 tablespoons tomato paste
- 1 teaspoon paprika
- 1 teaspoon ground cumin
- Salt and pepper to taste

For the filling:

- 1/2 lb (225g) ground beef or lamb
- 1 onion, finely chopped
- 2 tablespoons vegetable oil
- 1 teaspoon ground allspice
- Salt and pepper to taste
- Chopped parsley, for garnish
- Lemon wedges, for serving

Instructions:

1. In a large mixing bowl, combine the fine bulgur with hot water. Cover the bowl with a lid or plastic wrap and let it sit for about 15-20 minutes, or until the bulgur absorbs all the water and becomes soft.
2. In a separate skillet, heat the vegetable oil over medium heat. Add the finely chopped onion and sauté until softened and translucent, about 5 minutes.
3. Add the ground beef or lamb to the skillet and cook until browned, breaking it up with a spoon as it cooks.

4. Stir in the ground allspice, salt, and pepper to taste. Cook for another 2-3 minutes until the meat is cooked through. Remove the skillet from the heat and let the filling mixture cool slightly.
5. Once the bulgur is softened, add the finely chopped onion, tomato paste, paprika, ground cumin, salt, and pepper to the bulgur mixture. Mix well to combine.
6. Take a small portion of the bulgur mixture and flatten it in the palm of your hand. Place a spoonful of the meat filling in the center of the bulgur mixture.
7. Fold the edges of the bulgur mixture over the filling to enclose it completely, shaping it into a small patty or ball. Repeat with the remaining bulgur mixture and filling.
8. Heat some vegetable oil in a large skillet or frying pan over medium-high heat. Once the oil is hot, carefully add the bulgur köfte to the skillet in batches, making sure not to overcrowd the pan.
9. Fry the bulgur köfte for 3-4 minutes on each side, or until golden brown and crispy.
10. Once cooked, transfer the bulgur köfte to a plate lined with paper towels to drain any excess oil.
11. Serve the Turkish bulgur köfte hot, garnished with chopped parsley and lemon wedges on the side for squeezing over the köfte.

Enjoy these delicious and flavorful Turkish bulgur köfte as a main dish or appetizer with your favorite dipping sauce or yogurt on the side!

**Korean bibimbap**

Ingredients:

For the Bibimbap:

- 4 cups cooked short-grain white rice
- 1 cup spinach, washed and trimmed
- 1 cup bean sprouts
- 1 carrot, julienned
- 1 zucchini, julienned
- 4 shiitake mushrooms, sliced
- 1 cup mung bean sprouts
- 1 cup sliced cucumber
- 4 eggs
- Toasted sesame seeds, for garnish
- Thinly sliced green onions, for garnish
- Vegetable oil, for cooking
- Salt, to taste

For the Bibimbap Sauce:

- 1/4 cup gochujang (Korean red pepper paste)
- 2 tablespoons soy sauce
- 1 tablespoon sesame oil
- 1 tablespoon rice vinegar
- 1 tablespoon honey or sugar
- 2 cloves garlic, minced
- 1 teaspoon grated ginger
- 1 teaspoon toasted sesame seeds

Instructions:

1. Prepare the Bibimbap Sauce: In a small bowl, whisk together the gochujang, soy sauce, sesame oil, rice vinegar, honey or sugar, minced garlic, grated ginger, and toasted sesame seeds. Set aside.

2. Prepare the Vegetables: Blanch the spinach and bean sprouts separately in boiling water for about 1-2 minutes, then drain and squeeze out excess water. Season lightly with salt and set aside. Sauté the julienned carrot, zucchini, and shiitake mushrooms separately in a little vegetable oil until tender, then season lightly with salt and set aside. You can also blanch the mung bean sprouts briefly in boiling water, then drain and set aside. Slice the cucumber thinly and set aside.
3. Cook the Eggs: Heat a little vegetable oil in a non-stick skillet over medium heat. Crack the eggs into the skillet and fry them until the whites are set but the yolks are still runny. Cook to your desired doneness, then remove from heat and set aside.
4. Assemble the Bibimbap: Divide the cooked rice among serving bowls. Arrange the blanched spinach, sautéed vegetables, mung bean sprouts, sliced cucumber, and fried eggs on top of the rice in separate sections.
5. Serve the Bibimbap: Sprinkle toasted sesame seeds and thinly sliced green onions over the assembled bibimbap. Serve the bibimbap hot, with the bibimbap sauce on the side for drizzling over the top.
6. To eat, mix everything together thoroughly with the sauce before enjoying.

Enjoy this delicious and colorful Korean bibimbap as a satisfying and nutritious meal!

**French ratatouille with quinoa**

Ingredients:

For the Ratatouille:

- 1 eggplant, diced
- 2 zucchini, diced
- 1 yellow bell pepper, diced
- 1 red bell pepper, diced
- 1 onion, diced
- 2 cloves garlic, minced
- 2 tomatoes, diced
- 2 tablespoons tomato paste
- 2 tablespoons olive oil
- 1 teaspoon dried thyme
- 1 teaspoon dried oregano
- Salt and pepper to taste
- Fresh basil leaves, chopped, for garnish

For the Quinoa:

- 1 cup quinoa, rinsed
- 2 cups water or vegetable broth
- Salt to taste

Instructions:

1. Preheat the oven to 375°F (190°C).
2. In a large bowl, toss together the diced eggplant, zucchini, yellow bell pepper, red bell pepper, onion, and minced garlic with olive oil, dried thyme, dried oregano, salt, and pepper until evenly coated.
3. Spread the vegetable mixture in a single layer on a baking sheet lined with parchment paper. Roast in the preheated oven for 25-30 minutes, or until the vegetables are tender and slightly caramelized.
4. While the vegetables are roasting, rinse the quinoa under cold water until the water runs clear. In a medium saucepan, combine the rinsed quinoa with water or

vegetable broth and a pinch of salt. Bring to a boil, then reduce the heat to low, cover, and simmer for 15-20 minutes, or until the quinoa is cooked and the liquid is absorbed. Remove from heat and let it sit, covered, for 5 minutes. Fluff with a fork before serving.
5. In a large skillet, combine the roasted vegetables with diced tomatoes and tomato paste. Cook over medium heat for 5-10 minutes, stirring occasionally, until the flavors meld together and the mixture thickens slightly. Adjust seasoning with salt and pepper if needed.
6. Serve the ratatouille over cooked quinoa, garnished with freshly chopped basil leaves.

Enjoy this hearty and flavorful French ratatouille with quinoa as a nutritious and satisfying meal!

**Vietnamese spring rolls with rice vermicelli**

Ingredients:

For the Spring Rolls:

- 12 round rice paper wrappers (22cm diameter)
- 4 ounces (about 115g) rice vermicelli noodles
- 1 medium carrot, julienned
- 1 cucumber, julienned
- 1 red bell pepper, julienned
- 1 cup shredded lettuce or cabbage
- 1 cup fresh herbs (such as cilantro, mint, and Thai basil)
- 12 cooked shrimp, halved lengthwise (optional)
- 1/4 cup roasted peanuts, chopped (optional)
- Warm water, for softening rice paper wrappers

For the Dipping Sauce:

- 1/4 cup hoisin sauce
- 2 tablespoons peanut butter
- 2 tablespoons water
- 1 tablespoon soy sauce
- 1 tablespoon rice vinegar
- 1 teaspoon sriracha sauce (optional)
- 1 clove garlic, minced (optional)

Instructions:

1. Cook the rice vermicelli noodles according to the package instructions. Drain and rinse under cold water to stop the cooking process. Set aside.
2. Prepare all the vegetables and herbs, and arrange them on a plate or cutting board for easy assembly.
3. Fill a shallow dish or pie plate with warm water. Dip one rice paper wrapper into the water and rotate it gently until it softens, about 15-20 seconds. Place the softened wrapper on a clean, damp kitchen towel or a plate.

4. Arrange a small amount of cooked rice vermicelli noodles in the center of the softened rice paper wrapper, leaving about 2 inches of space on each side.
5. Layer the julienned vegetables, shredded lettuce or cabbage, fresh herbs, and cooked shrimp (if using) on top of the rice noodles.
6. Fold the bottom edge of the rice paper wrapper over the filling, then fold in the sides, and roll tightly to enclose the filling. Repeat with the remaining ingredients to make more spring rolls.
7. To make the dipping sauce, whisk together hoisin sauce, peanut butter, water, soy sauce, rice vinegar, sriracha sauce (if using), and minced garlic (if using) until smooth. Adjust the consistency with more water if needed.
8. Serve the Vietnamese spring rolls with rice vermicelli immediately with the dipping sauce on the side. Sprinkle chopped roasted peanuts on top for added flavor and texture, if desired.

Enjoy these fresh and flavorful Vietnamese spring rolls with rice vermicelli as a light appetizer or snack!

## Hawaiian poi

Ingredients:

- 2-3 medium taro roots
- Water

Instructions:

1. Choose fresh, firm taro roots. Rinse them under cold water to remove any dirt.
2. Peel the taro roots with a vegetable peeler or knife, being careful to remove the tough outer layer.
3. Cut the peeled taro roots into small cubes or chunks.
4. Place the cubed taro roots in a large pot and cover them with water.
5. Bring the water to a boil over medium-high heat, then reduce the heat to low and simmer the taro roots until they are tender, about 20-30 minutes.
6. Drain the cooked taro roots and transfer them to a food processor or blender.
7. Add a small amount of water to the taro roots in the food processor or blender, then process or blend until smooth and creamy. Add more water as needed to achieve the desired consistency.
8. Once the taro roots are pureed into a smooth paste, transfer the mixture to a clean pot.
9. Cook the taro paste over low heat, stirring constantly, until it thickens to the consistency of pudding, about 10-15 minutes. Be careful not to let it burn.
10. Remove the pot from the heat and let the poi cool slightly before serving.
11. Serve the Hawaiian poi warm or at room temperature.

Hawaiian poi is traditionally eaten with the fingers and has a slightly tangy flavor. It can be enjoyed on its own or as a side dish with other Hawaiian foods such as kalua pig, lomi lomi salmon, or laulau. Enjoy this traditional Hawaiian delicacy as a unique and nutritious part of your meal!

**Israeli couscous salad**

Ingredients:

For the Salad:

- 1 cup Israeli couscous (pearl couscous)
- 1 1/4 cups water or vegetable broth
- 1 cup cherry tomatoes, halved
- 1 cucumber, diced
- 1/2 red onion, finely chopped
- 1/4 cup Kalamata olives, pitted and sliced
- 1/4 cup fresh parsley, chopped
- 1/4 cup fresh mint leaves, chopped
- 1/4 cup crumbled feta cheese (optional)
- Salt and pepper to taste

For the Dressing:

- 3 tablespoons extra-virgin olive oil
- 2 tablespoons lemon juice
- 1 tablespoon red wine vinegar
- 1 teaspoon Dijon mustard
- 1 clove garlic, minced
- Salt and pepper to taste

Instructions:

1. In a medium saucepan, bring the water or vegetable broth to a boil. Add the Israeli couscous and a pinch of salt. Reduce the heat to low, cover, and simmer for 10-12 minutes, or until the couscous is tender and all the liquid is absorbed. Remove from heat and let it cool to room temperature.
2. In a large mixing bowl, combine the cooked Israeli couscous with the halved cherry tomatoes, diced cucumber, finely chopped red onion, sliced Kalamata

olives, chopped parsley, chopped mint leaves, and crumbled feta cheese (if using).
3. In a small bowl, whisk together the extra-virgin olive oil, lemon juice, red wine vinegar, Dijon mustard, minced garlic, salt, and pepper to make the dressing.
4. Pour the dressing over the Israeli couscous salad and toss gently to coat all the ingredients evenly.
5. Taste and adjust the seasoning with more salt and pepper if needed.
6. Cover the salad and refrigerate for at least 30 minutes to allow the flavors to meld together.
7. Before serving, give the Israeli couscous salad a final toss and garnish with additional chopped herbs if desired.
8. Serve the Israeli couscous salad chilled or at room temperature as a delicious side dish or light meal.

This Israeli couscous salad is perfect for picnics, potlucks, or as a refreshing addition to your summer menu. Enjoy its vibrant flavors and textures!

**German spaetzle with cheese sauce**

Ingredients:

For the Spaetzle:

- 2 cups all-purpose flour
- 4 large eggs
- 1/2 cup milk
- 1/2 teaspoon salt
- 1/4 teaspoon ground nutmeg
- Water, for boiling

For the Cheese Sauce:

- 2 tablespoons unsalted butter
- 2 tablespoons all-purpose flour
- 1 cup milk
- 1 cup shredded cheese (such as Swiss, Gruyere, or Emmental)
- Salt and pepper to taste
- Chopped fresh parsley, for garnish (optional)

Instructions:

1. In a large mixing bowl, combine the all-purpose flour, eggs, milk, salt, and ground nutmeg. Stir until a smooth batter forms. The batter should have a thick, but pourable consistency.
2. Bring a large pot of salted water to a boil.
3. To make the spaetzle, hold a colander or spaetzle maker over the boiling water. Pour a ladleful of batter into the colander or spaetzle maker, and using a rubber spatula or the back of a spoon, press the batter through the holes into the boiling water. Work in batches to avoid overcrowding the pot.
4. Cook the spaetzle for about 2-3 minutes, or until they float to the surface of the water. Use a slotted spoon to transfer the cooked spaetzle to a colander to drain. Repeat the process with the remaining batter.

5. Meanwhile, in a separate saucepan, melt the butter over medium heat. Add the all-purpose flour and cook, stirring constantly, for 1-2 minutes to make a roux.
6. Gradually whisk in the milk, stirring constantly to prevent lumps from forming. Cook the sauce until it thickens, about 3-5 minutes.
7. Reduce the heat to low and stir in the shredded cheese until melted and smooth. Season the cheese sauce with salt and pepper to taste.
8. Add the cooked spaetzle to the cheese sauce and toss gently to coat all the noodles evenly.
9. Serve the German spaetzle with cheese sauce hot, garnished with chopped fresh parsley if desired.

Enjoy this hearty and comforting German dish as a main course or side dish. It's perfect for a cozy family dinner or a special occasion!

**Bangladeshi khichuri**

Ingredients:

- 1 cup basmati rice
- 1/2 cup yellow split lentils (moong dal)
- 1 onion, thinly sliced
- 2 cloves garlic, minced
- 1-inch piece of ginger, grated
- 2-3 green chilies, chopped (adjust to taste)
- 1 teaspoon cumin seeds
- 1 cinnamon stick
- 2-3 cardamom pods
- 2-3 cloves
- 1 bay leaf
- 1/2 teaspoon turmeric powder
- 1/2 teaspoon chili powder (optional)
- Salt to taste
- 3 cups water
- 2 tablespoons vegetable oil or ghee
- Fresh cilantro leaves, chopped, for garnish (optional)
- Lemon wedges, for serving

Instructions:

1. Rinse the basmati rice and yellow split lentils (moong dal) under cold water until the water runs clear. Drain and set aside.
2. In a large pot or pressure cooker, heat the vegetable oil or ghee over medium heat. Add the cumin seeds, cinnamon stick, cardamom pods, cloves, and bay leaf. Fry for a minute or until fragrant.
3. Add the thinly sliced onion to the pot and sauté until golden brown.
4. Stir in the minced garlic, grated ginger, and chopped green chilies. Sauté for another minute until fragrant.
5. Add the rinsed basmati rice and yellow split lentils to the pot. Stir to coat the grains with the spices and onions.
6. Season with turmeric powder, chili powder (if using), and salt to taste. Mix well.
7. Pour in the water and give everything a good stir. Bring the mixture to a boil.

8. Once boiling, reduce the heat to low, cover the pot, and let the khichuri simmer for about 20-25 minutes, or until the rice and lentils are cooked and the mixture is creamy. If using a pressure cooker, cook for about 2-3 whistles.
9. Once the khichuri is cooked, remove it from the heat and let it sit for a few minutes before serving.
10. Serve the Bangladeshi khichuri hot, garnished with chopped fresh cilantro leaves if desired. Serve with lemon wedges on the side for squeezing over the khichuri.

Enjoy this comforting and flavorful Bangladeshi khichuri as a nourishing meal on its own or accompanied by your favorite side dishes!

**Venezuelan arepas**

Ingredients:

- 2 cups pre-cooked white cornmeal (such as Harina P.A.N. or Masarepa)
- 1 1/2 to 2 cups warm water
- 1 teaspoon salt
- Vegetable oil, for cooking

Instructions:

1. In a mixing bowl, combine the pre-cooked white cornmeal and salt.
2. Gradually add warm water, starting with 1 1/2 cups, and mix with your hands until a soft and smooth dough forms. The dough should be moist but not too sticky. If needed, add more water, a little at a time, until you reach the right consistency.
3. Let the dough rest for about 5 minutes to allow the cornmeal to fully hydrate.
4. Divide the dough into equal-sized portions and shape each portion into a ball.
5. Flatten each ball into a disc shape, about 1/2 to 3/4 inch thick, using your hands. Make sure the edges are smooth and even.
6. Heat a non-stick skillet or griddle over medium heat and lightly grease it with vegetable oil.
7. Place the formed arepas on the skillet or griddle and cook for about 5-7 minutes on each side, or until golden brown and crispy. You may need to adjust the heat to prevent burning.
8. Once cooked, transfer the arepas to a plate lined with paper towels to absorb any excess oil.
9. Let the arepas cool slightly before slicing them open horizontally with a knife, being careful not to cut all the way through.
10. Fill the sliced arepas with your favorite fillings, such as shredded beef, chicken, black beans, cheese, avocado, or any other toppings you prefer.
11. Serve the filled arepas warm and enjoy!

These arepas are best enjoyed fresh and warm, but you can also store any leftovers in an airtight container in the refrigerator and reheat them in a toaster or oven before serving. Enjoy your homemade Venezuelan arepas!

**Finnish rye bread with smoked salmon**

Ingredients:

For the Finnish Rye Bread:

- 2 cups rye flour
- 1 cup all-purpose flour
- 1 1/2 cups lukewarm water
- 1 packet (7g) active dry yeast
- 1 tablespoon honey or sugar
- 1 teaspoon salt
- 1 tablespoon caraway seeds (optional)
- Cornmeal or additional rye flour, for dusting

For Serving:

- Smoked salmon slices
- Cream cheese or sour cream
- Fresh dill, chopped
- Lemon wedges

Instructions:

1. In a small bowl, dissolve the honey or sugar in the lukewarm water. Sprinkle the active dry yeast over the water and let it sit for about 5-10 minutes, or until frothy.
2. In a large mixing bowl, combine the rye flour, all-purpose flour, salt, and caraway seeds (if using). Stir to mix well.
3. Gradually add the yeast mixture to the flour mixture, stirring with a wooden spoon until a sticky dough forms.
4. Turn the dough out onto a floured surface and knead for about 5-7 minutes, or until the dough becomes smooth and elastic.
5. Shape the dough into a ball and place it in a lightly greased bowl. Cover the bowl with a clean kitchen towel or plastic wrap and let the dough rise in a warm, draft-free place for about 1-2 hours, or until doubled in size.
6. Preheat your oven to 400°F (200°C). Place a baking stone or inverted baking sheet in the oven to preheat.

7. Punch down the risen dough and transfer it to a lightly floured surface. Shape the dough into a round loaf and place it on a piece of parchment paper dusted with cornmeal or additional rye flour.
8. Cover the loaf loosely with a clean kitchen towel and let it rise for another 30-45 minutes, or until slightly puffed.
9. Using a sharp knife, make shallow slashes on the surface of the loaf.
10. Transfer the loaf to the preheated baking stone or baking sheet and bake for 30-35 minutes, or until the bread is golden brown and sounds hollow when tapped on the bottom.
11. Remove the bread from the oven and let it cool completely on a wire rack before slicing.
12. To serve, slice the Finnish rye bread and top each slice with smoked salmon, a dollop of cream cheese or sour cream, and a sprinkle of fresh chopped dill. Serve with lemon wedges on the side.

Enjoy this delicious Finnish rye bread with smoked salmon as a light and flavorful snack or appetizer!

**Cuban moros y cristianos (black beans and rice)**

Ingredients:

For the Black Beans:

- 1 cup dried black beans
- 4 cups water
- 1 onion, chopped
- 4 cloves garlic, minced
- 1 green bell pepper, chopped
- 1 bay leaf
- 1 teaspoon ground cumin
- Salt and pepper to taste

For the Rice:

- 1 cup long-grain white rice
- 2 cups water or vegetable broth
- 1 tablespoon olive oil
- 1 onion, chopped
- 2 cloves garlic, minced
- 1 bell pepper (any color), chopped
- 1 teaspoon ground cumin
- Salt and pepper to taste
- Fresh cilantro or parsley, chopped, for garnish (optional)

Instructions:

1. Start by preparing the black beans. Rinse the dried black beans under cold water and remove any debris or stones.
2. In a large pot, combine the rinsed black beans, water, chopped onion, minced garlic, chopped green bell pepper, bay leaf, ground cumin, salt, and pepper.
3. Bring the mixture to a boil over high heat, then reduce the heat to low and simmer, covered, for about 1 to 1 1/2 hours, or until the beans are tender. Stir occasionally and add more water if needed to keep the beans submerged.

4. Once the black beans are tender, remove the bay leaf and adjust the seasoning with more salt and pepper if needed. Keep the beans warm while you prepare the rice.
5. To make the rice, heat olive oil in a large skillet or pot over medium heat. Add the chopped onion, minced garlic, and chopped bell pepper. Sauté until the vegetables are softened, about 5 minutes.
6. Stir in the ground cumin and rice, and cook for another 2-3 minutes, stirring frequently.
7. Pour in the water or vegetable broth and season with salt and pepper to taste. Bring the mixture to a boil, then reduce the heat to low and cover the pot. Let the rice simmer for about 18-20 minutes, or until the liquid is absorbed and the rice is cooked through.
8. Once the rice is cooked, fluff it with a fork and remove it from the heat.
9. To serve, spoon a generous portion of the black beans over the cooked rice. Garnish with fresh chopped cilantro or parsley if desired.
10. Serve the Cuban moros y cristianos hot as a delicious and satisfying meal.

Enjoy the rich flavors and comforting textures of this classic Cuban dish!

**Thai mango sticky rice**

Ingredients:

For the Sticky Rice:

- 1 cup glutinous rice (also known as sweet rice or sticky rice)
- 1 cup coconut milk
- 1/2 cup water
- 1/4 cup granulated sugar
- 1/2 teaspoon salt

For Serving:

- 2 ripe mangoes, peeled and sliced
- 1/2 cup coconut milk
- 2 tablespoons granulated sugar
- Toasted sesame seeds or toasted mung beans (optional), for garnish

Instructions:

1. Rinse the glutinous rice under cold water until the water runs clear. Soak the rice in enough water to cover it for at least 4 hours or overnight.
2. Drain the soaked rice and transfer it to a steamer basket lined with cheesecloth or a clean kitchen towel. Steam the rice over boiling water for about 25-30 minutes, or until the rice is tender and cooked through.
3. While the rice is steaming, prepare the coconut sauce. In a small saucepan, combine the coconut milk, granulated sugar, and salt. Heat the mixture over medium heat, stirring constantly, until the sugar is dissolved and the sauce is smooth. Remove from heat and let it cool to room temperature.
4. Once the rice is cooked, transfer it to a mixing bowl and gently fluff it with a fork or spatula.
5. Pour about half of the coconut sauce over the cooked sticky rice and gently fold it in until the rice is evenly coated. Reserve the remaining sauce for serving.

6. To serve, spoon a portion of the sticky rice onto serving plates or bowls. Arrange slices of ripe mango alongside the rice.
7. Drizzle the remaining coconut sauce over the sticky rice and mango slices.
8. If desired, sprinkle toasted sesame seeds or toasted mung beans over the top for added flavor and texture.
9. Serve the Thai mango sticky rice immediately and enjoy the delicious combination of flavors and textures!

Thai mango sticky rice is best enjoyed fresh, but any leftovers can be stored in an airtight container in the refrigerator for up to 2 days. Simply reheat gently before serving.

**Afghan rice pilaf with raisins and carrots**

Ingredients:

- 2 cups basmati rice, rinsed and soaked for 30 minutes
- 4 cups water
- 1 onion, thinly sliced
- 2 carrots, peeled and julienned
- 1/2 cup raisins
- 1/4 cup vegetable oil or ghee
- 1 teaspoon cumin seeds
- 1 teaspoon ground cardamom
- 1/2 teaspoon ground cinnamon
- Salt to taste
- Slivered almonds or chopped pistachios, for garnish (optional)
- Fresh cilantro or parsley, chopped, for garnish (optional)

Instructions:

1. In a large pot, heat the vegetable oil or ghee over medium heat. Add the sliced onion and cook until golden brown and caramelized, stirring occasionally.
2. Add the julienned carrots to the pot and sauté for a few minutes until they begin to soften.
3. Stir in the raisins, cumin seeds, ground cardamom, and ground cinnamon. Cook for another minute to toast the spices and allow the flavors to meld together.
4. Drain the soaked rice and add it to the pot. Stir well to coat the rice with the onion, carrot, and spice mixture.
5. Pour in the water and season with salt to taste. Bring the mixture to a boil, then reduce the heat to low, cover the pot, and simmer for about 15-20 minutes, or until the rice is tender and all the water is absorbed.
6. Once the rice is cooked, remove the pot from the heat and let it sit, covered, for another 5-10 minutes to steam.
7. Fluff the rice with a fork to separate the grains and evenly distribute the carrots and raisins throughout.
8. Transfer the Afghan rice pilaf to a serving platter and garnish with slivered almonds or chopped pistachios and fresh chopped cilantro or parsley, if desired.

9. Serve the rice pilaf warm as a delicious and aromatic side dish to accompany your favorite Afghan main courses.

Enjoy the fragrant aroma and delightful flavors of this Afghan rice pilaf with raisins and carrots!

**Polish pierogi with buckwheat filling**

Ingredients:

For the Pierogi Dough:

- 2 cups all-purpose flour, plus extra for dusting
- 1 large egg
- 1/2 cup sour cream
- 1/4 cup unsalted butter, melted
- 1/4 teaspoon salt

For the Buckwheat Filling:

- 1 cup buckwheat groats
- 2 cups water
- 1 tablespoon unsalted butter
- 1 small onion, finely chopped
- Salt and pepper to taste

Instructions:

1. Start by preparing the buckwheat filling. Rinse the buckwheat groats under cold water and drain well.
2. In a medium saucepan, bring the water to a boil. Add the rinsed buckwheat groats and a pinch of salt. Reduce the heat to low, cover, and simmer for about 10-12 minutes, or until the buckwheat is tender and the water is absorbed. Remove from heat and let it cool slightly.
3. In a skillet, melt the butter over medium heat. Add the finely chopped onion and sauté until softened and translucent, about 5 minutes.
4. Add the cooked buckwheat to the skillet with the onions. Season with salt and pepper to taste. Cook for another 2-3 minutes, stirring occasionally, until the flavors are well combined. Remove from heat and let the filling cool completely.
5. To make the pierogi dough, in a large mixing bowl, combine the flour and salt. Make a well in the center and add the egg, sour cream, and melted butter.
6. Use a fork or your hands to gradually incorporate the wet ingredients into the flour until a dough forms. Knead the dough on a lightly floured surface for about

5 minutes, or until smooth and elastic. If the dough is too sticky, add a little more flour as needed.
7. Divide the dough into two equal portions. Roll out one portion of the dough on a floured surface to about 1/8 inch thickness.
8. Use a round cookie cutter or a glass to cut out circles of dough. Place a teaspoon of the cooled buckwheat filling in the center of each dough circle.
9. Fold the dough over the filling to form a half-moon shape. Press the edges together firmly to seal, then crimp the edges with a fork to ensure they are tightly sealed.
10. Repeat the process with the remaining dough and filling.
11. Bring a large pot of salted water to a boil. Carefully drop the pierogi into the boiling water, a few at a time, making sure not to overcrowd the pot. Cook for about 3-4 minutes, or until the pierogi float to the surface and are cooked through.
12. Use a slotted spoon to remove the cooked pierogi from the water and transfer them to a plate lined with paper towels to drain.
13. Serve the Polish pierogi with buckwheat filling hot, with sour cream or melted butter for dipping, and garnish with chopped fresh herbs if desired.

Enjoy these homemade Polish pierogi with buckwheat filling as a comforting and delicious meal!

**Canadian maple syrup oatmeal**

Ingredients:

- 1 cup rolled oats
- 2 cups water or milk (or a combination of both)
- Pinch of salt
- 2-3 tablespoons Canadian maple syrup (adjust to taste)
- Optional toppings: sliced bananas, chopped nuts, fresh berries, cinnamon

Instructions:

1. In a saucepan, bring the water or milk to a boil over medium-high heat.
2. Stir in the rolled oats and a pinch of salt. Reduce the heat to medium-low and simmer, stirring occasionally, for about 5 minutes, or until the oats are cooked and the mixture has thickened to your desired consistency.
3. Remove the saucepan from the heat and stir in the Canadian maple syrup, adjusting the amount to your taste preferences.
4. Let the oatmeal stand for a minute or two to allow the flavors to meld together.
5. Serve the Canadian maple syrup oatmeal hot, topped with your favorite toppings such as sliced bananas, chopped nuts, fresh berries, or a sprinkle of cinnamon.
6. Enjoy this warm and comforting breakfast on a chilly Canadian morning, or any time you're craving a delicious and nutritious meal!

Feel free to customize this recipe by adding your favorite toppings or adjusting the sweetness level to suit your taste.

**Belgian waffles with berries**

Ingredients:

For the Waffles:

- 2 cups all-purpose flour
- 2 tablespoons granulated sugar
- 1 tablespoon baking powder
- 1/2 teaspoon salt
- 2 large eggs
- 1 3/4 cups milk
- 1/2 cup unsalted butter, melted
- 1 teaspoon vanilla extract

For Serving:

- Fresh mixed berries (such as strawberries, blueberries, raspberries, and blackberries)
- Maple syrup or honey
- Whipped cream (optional)

Instructions:

1. Preheat your Belgian waffle maker according to the manufacturer's instructions.
2. In a large mixing bowl, whisk together the all-purpose flour, granulated sugar, baking powder, and salt.
3. In a separate bowl, beat the eggs. Add the milk, melted butter, and vanilla extract, and whisk until well combined.
4. Pour the wet ingredients into the dry ingredients and stir until just combined. Be careful not to overmix; a few lumps are okay.
5. Lightly grease the waffle maker with cooking spray or brush with melted butter.
6. Pour enough batter onto the center of the preheated waffle maker to cover about two-thirds of the waffle grid. Close the lid and cook according to the manufacturer's instructions, or until the waffles are golden brown and crisp.

7. Carefully remove the cooked waffles from the waffle maker and transfer them to a serving plate.
8. Top the Belgian waffles with fresh mixed berries.
9. Drizzle maple syrup or honey over the waffles and berries.
10. Optionally, add a dollop of whipped cream on top.
11. Serve the Belgian waffles with berries immediately while they are warm and enjoy the delicious combination of flavors!

These Belgian waffles with berries are perfect for a leisurely weekend breakfast or brunch, and they're sure to impress your family and friends!

**Dutch poffertjes (mini pancakes)**

Ingredients:

- 1 cup all-purpose flour
- 1 tablespoon granulated sugar
- 1 teaspoon instant yeast
- 1/2 teaspoon salt
- 1 cup milk, warmed to about 110°F (45°C)
- 1 large egg
- 1 tablespoon unsalted butter, melted
- Butter or vegetable oil, for greasing the pan
- Powdered sugar, for dusting
- Optional toppings: Nutella, maple syrup, fresh berries, whipped cream

Special equipment: Poffertjes pan (or a mini pancake pan)

Instructions:

1. In a large mixing bowl, whisk together the all-purpose flour, granulated sugar, instant yeast, and salt.
2. In a separate bowl, whisk together the warm milk, egg, and melted butter.
3. Gradually pour the wet ingredients into the dry ingredients, whisking continuously until you have a smooth batter. The batter should be thick but pourable. If it's too thick, you can add a little more warm milk to reach the desired consistency.
4. Cover the bowl with plastic wrap or a clean kitchen towel and let the batter rest in a warm place for about 30-45 minutes, or until it becomes slightly bubbly and doubles in volume.
5. While the batter is resting, preheat your poffertjes pan over medium-low heat. Lightly grease each indent in the pan with butter or vegetable oil.
6. Once the pan is hot, pour a small amount of batter into each indent, filling them about three-quarters full.
7. Cook the poffertjes for about 2-3 minutes, or until bubbles form on the surface and the bottoms are golden brown. Use a skewer or fork to carefully flip each poffertje over.

8. Continue cooking for another 1-2 minutes, or until the other side is golden brown and the poffertjes are cooked through.
9. Transfer the cooked poffertjes to a plate and keep them warm while you cook the remaining batter. You may need to regrease the pan between batches.
10. Once all the poffertjes are cooked, dust them generously with powdered sugar.
11. Serve the Dutch poffertjes warm with your favorite toppings, such as Nutella, maple syrup, fresh berries, or whipped cream.

Enjoy these fluffy and delicious Dutch poffertjes as a special treat for breakfast, brunch, or dessert!

**Malaysian nasi lemak**

Ingredients:

For the Coconut Rice:

- 2 cups jasmine rice
- 1 3/4 cups coconut milk
- 1 cup water
- 2 pandan leaves, tied into knots (optional)
- 1 teaspoon salt

For the Sambal (Spicy Chili Paste):

- 10-12 dried red chilies, soaked in hot water and deseeded
- 4 shallots, roughly chopped
- 3 cloves garlic, roughly chopped
- 1 inch ginger, peeled and roughly chopped
- 2 tablespoons dried shrimp (optional)
- 2 tablespoons vegetable oil
- 2 tablespoons tamarind paste
- 2 tablespoons palm sugar or brown sugar
- Salt to taste

For the Accompaniments:

- Hard-boiled eggs, halved
- Cucumber slices
- Fried anchovies (ikan bilis)
- Fried peanuts
- Slices of fried or grilled chicken (optional)
- Slices of fried fish (optional)
- Slices of fried tempeh or tofu (optional)
- Fresh cilantro or Thai basil leaves (optional)
- Slices of fresh lime or calamansi (optional)

Instructions:

1. Rinse the jasmine rice under cold water until the water runs clear. Drain well.
2. In a rice cooker or a medium pot, combine the rinsed rice, coconut milk, water, pandan leaves (if using), and salt. Stir well to combine.
3. Cook the rice according to your rice cooker's instructions or bring the pot to a boil, then reduce the heat to low, cover, and simmer for about 15-20 minutes, or until the rice is cooked and the liquid is absorbed. Fluff the rice with a fork and remove the pandan leaves before serving.
4. While the rice is cooking, prepare the sambal. In a blender or food processor, combine the soaked and deseeded dried red chilies, shallots, garlic, ginger, and dried shrimp (if using). Blend until you get a smooth paste, adding a little water if needed to facilitate blending.
5. Heat the vegetable oil in a skillet or wok over medium heat. Add the blended chili paste and cook, stirring frequently, for about 5-7 minutes, or until fragrant and the oil starts to separate.
6. Stir in the tamarind paste and palm sugar (or brown sugar). Cook for another 5-7 minutes, or until the sambal thickens. Season with salt to taste. Remove from heat and set aside.
7. Prepare the accompaniments by frying the anchovies and peanuts until crispy, slicing the cucumber, and halving the hard-boiled eggs.
8. To serve, spoon some coconut rice onto serving plates. Top with a dollop of sambal and arrange the desired accompaniments around the rice.
9. Garnish with fresh cilantro or Thai basil leaves, if using, and serve with slices of fresh lime or calamansi on the side.

Enjoy this flavorful and aromatic Malaysian nasi lemak as a delicious meal any time of the day!

**Georgian khachapuri (cheese bread)**

Ingredients:

For the Dough:

- 2 cups all-purpose flour
- 1 teaspoon active dry yeast
- 1 teaspoon sugar
- 1/2 teaspoon salt
- 3/4 cup warm water
- 2 tablespoons vegetable oil

For the Filling:

- 2 cups shredded mozzarella cheese
- 1 cup crumbled feta cheese
- 1 egg
- 2 tablespoons butter, diced into small cubes
- Additional egg, for topping (optional)
- Additional butter, for topping (optional)

Instructions:

1. In a small bowl, combine the warm water, sugar, and active dry yeast. Let it sit for about 5-10 minutes, or until frothy.
2. In a large mixing bowl, combine the flour and salt. Add the yeast mixture and vegetable oil to the flour mixture. Mix until a dough forms.
3. Turn the dough out onto a floured surface and knead for about 5-7 minutes, or until the dough is smooth and elastic. Place the dough in a greased bowl, cover with a clean kitchen towel, and let it rise in a warm place for about 1-2 hours, or until doubled in size.
4. Preheat your oven to 475°F (245°C). If you have a pizza stone, place it in the oven to preheat as well.

5. Punch down the risen dough and divide it into two equal portions. Roll out each portion into an oval shape, about 1/4 inch thick.
6. Place half of the shredded mozzarella cheese and crumbled feta cheese in the center of each oval-shaped dough, leaving a border around the edges.
7. Fold the edges of the dough over the cheese filling, pinching and twisting to create a boat shape with an opening in the center.
8. Crack an egg into the center of each khachapuri boat. Scatter diced butter over the cheese and egg.
9. Carefully transfer the khachapuri onto a baking sheet lined with parchment paper or onto the preheated pizza stone in the oven.
10. Bake for about 12-15 minutes, or until the crust is golden brown and the cheese is melted and bubbly.
11. Optional: If desired, crack an additional egg into the center of each khachapuri boat during the last few minutes of baking to cook the egg further.
12. Remove the khachapuri from the oven and let them cool slightly before serving.
13. Serve the Georgian khachapuri hot, with additional butter on top if desired. Enjoy the cheesy goodness!

This Georgian khachapuri recipe makes a delicious and comforting dish that's perfect for sharing with family and friends.

**Filipino arroz caldo (rice porridge)**

Ingredients:

- 1 cup glutinous rice (malagkit) or jasmine rice, rinsed and drained
- 1 tablespoon vegetable oil
- 1 onion, finely chopped
- 4 cloves garlic, minced
- 1 thumb-sized piece of ginger, peeled and minced
- 1 lb (450g) chicken thighs or breast, cut into bite-sized pieces
- 6 cups chicken broth or water
- 1 teaspoon fish sauce (patis) or to taste
- Salt and pepper to taste
- Optional toppings: sliced hard-boiled eggs, chopped green onions, fried garlic, calamansi or lemon wedges

Instructions:

1. Heat the vegetable oil in a large pot over medium heat. Add the chopped onion and cook until softened, about 3-4 minutes.
2. Add the minced garlic and ginger to the pot and cook for another 1-2 minutes, until fragrant.
3. Add the chicken pieces to the pot and cook until they are lightly browned on all sides, about 5-7 minutes.
4. Pour in the chicken broth or water and bring the mixture to a boil.
5. Once boiling, add the rinsed and drained glutinous rice or jasmine rice to the pot. Stir well to combine.
6. Lower the heat to medium-low and let the Arroz Caldo simmer, stirring occasionally, until the rice is cooked and the porridge has thickened to your desired consistency, about 30-40 minutes.
7. Season the Arroz Caldo with fish sauce (patis), salt, and pepper to taste. Adjust the seasoning as needed.
8. Ladle the Arroz Caldo into serving bowls and top with your choice of optional toppings, such as sliced hard-boiled eggs, chopped green onions, fried garlic, and calamansi or lemon wedges.
9. Serve the Filipino Arroz Caldo hot and enjoy its comforting and nourishing flavors!

Arroz Caldo is often served as a filling meal on its own or as a comforting dish when someone is feeling under the weather. It's also commonly enjoyed during breakfast or merienda (snack) time in the Philippines.

**Sri Lankan coconut roti**

Ingredients:

- 2 cups all-purpose flour
- 1 cup grated coconut (fresh or desiccated)
- 1 small onion, finely chopped
- 1 green chili, finely chopped (optional, for added heat)
- 1/4 cup chopped fresh cilantro or curry leaves (optional, for added flavor)
- 1/2 teaspoon salt, or to taste
- Water, as needed
- Vegetable oil or ghee, for cooking

Instructions:

1. In a large mixing bowl, combine the all-purpose flour, grated coconut, chopped onion, chopped green chili (if using), chopped cilantro or curry leaves (if using), and salt. Mix well to combine all the ingredients.
2. Gradually add water to the flour mixture, a little at a time, and knead to form a smooth and pliable dough. The dough should hold together well but not be too sticky. Adjust the amount of water as needed.
3. Divide the dough into small balls, about the size of a golf ball.
4. Heat a griddle or non-stick skillet over medium heat and lightly grease it with vegetable oil or ghee.
5. Take one dough ball and flatten it into a disc using your hands. Alternatively, you can roll it out with a rolling pin on a floured surface to about 1/4 inch thickness.
6. Carefully transfer the flattened dough to the heated griddle or skillet.
7. Cook the roti for about 2-3 minutes on each side, or until golden brown and cooked through. Brush a little vegetable oil or ghee on top of each roti while cooking for added flavor and crispiness.
8. Repeat the process with the remaining dough balls, flattening them into discs and cooking them on the griddle or skillet until all the roti are cooked.
9. Serve the Sri Lankan coconut roti hot with your favorite curry, chutney, or sambal.

Enjoy the delicious flavor and texture of Sri Lankan coconut roti as a tasty accompaniment to your meals or as a snack on its own!

**Tunisian couscous with lamb**

Ingredients:

For the Lamb:

- 1 lb (450g) lamb shoulder or leg, cut into bite-sized pieces
- 2 tablespoons olive oil
- 1 onion, finely chopped
- 2 cloves garlic, minced
- 1 teaspoon ground cumin
- 1 teaspoon ground coriander
- 1 teaspoon paprika
- 1/2 teaspoon ground cinnamon
- Salt and pepper to taste
- 2 cups chicken or lamb broth
- 1 can (14 oz) diced tomatoes

For the Couscous:

- 2 cups couscous
- 2 cups chicken or lamb broth
- 2 tablespoons olive oil
- Salt to taste

For Serving:

- Chopped fresh cilantro or parsley, for garnish
- Lemon wedges, for serving

Instructions:

1. In a large pot or Dutch oven, heat the olive oil over medium heat. Add the chopped onion and cook until softened, about 5 minutes.
2. Add the minced garlic to the pot and cook for another 1-2 minutes, until fragrant.

3. Add the lamb pieces to the pot and season with ground cumin, ground coriander, paprika, ground cinnamon, salt, and pepper. Cook until the lamb is browned on all sides.
4. Pour in the chicken or lamb broth and diced tomatoes. Bring the mixture to a simmer, then reduce the heat to low. Cover and cook for about 1 to 1 1/2 hours, or until the lamb is tender and cooked through. Stir occasionally and add more broth if needed to prevent the mixture from drying out.
5. While the lamb is cooking, prepare the couscous. In a separate saucepan, bring the chicken or lamb broth to a boil. Stir in the couscous and olive oil. Remove from heat, cover, and let it sit for about 5 minutes, or until the couscous has absorbed all the liquid. Fluff the couscous with a fork.
6. Once the lamb is cooked and tender, adjust the seasoning of the sauce with salt and pepper to taste.
7. To serve, spoon the cooked couscous onto serving plates or bowls. Top with the Tunisian lamb stew and garnish with chopped fresh cilantro or parsley. Serve with lemon wedges on the side for squeezing over the couscous and lamb.
8. Enjoy the Tunisian couscous with lamb hot, and savor the rich flavors and tender texture of this comforting dish!

This Tunisian couscous with lamb is sure to be a hit at any dinner table, and it's perfect for sharing with family and friends.

**Hungarian goulash with barley**

Ingredients:

- 1 lb (450g) beef stew meat, cut into bite-sized pieces
- 2 tablespoons vegetable oil
- 1 onion, chopped
- 2 cloves garlic, minced
- 2 carrots, peeled and diced
- 2 celery stalks, diced
- 2 tablespoons tomato paste
- 1 tablespoon paprika
- 1 teaspoon caraway seeds
- 4 cups beef broth
- 1 cup pearl barley
- Salt and pepper to taste
- Chopped fresh parsley, for garnish

Instructions:

1. In a large pot or Dutch oven, heat the vegetable oil over medium-high heat. Add the beef stew meat and cook until browned on all sides. Remove the beef from the pot and set it aside.
2. In the same pot, add the chopped onion and cook until softened, about 5 minutes.
3. Add the minced garlic, diced carrots, and diced celery to the pot. Cook for another 3-4 minutes, until the vegetables are slightly softened.
4. Stir in the tomato paste, paprika, and caraway seeds, and cook for 1-2 minutes, until fragrant.
5. Return the browned beef to the pot. Pour in the beef broth and bring the mixture to a boil.
6. Once boiling, reduce the heat to low and cover the pot. Let the goulash simmer for about 1 to 1 1/2 hours, or until the beef is tender.
7. While the goulash is simmering, rinse the pearl barley under cold water and drain well.
8. After the beef has cooked for about 1 hour, add the rinsed pearl barley to the pot. Stir well to combine.

9. Continue to simmer the goulash for another 30-40 minutes, or until the barley is tender and cooked through. If the mixture becomes too thick, you can add more beef broth or water as needed.
10. Season the goulash with salt and pepper to taste.
11. Once the goulash is ready, ladle it into serving bowls and garnish with chopped fresh parsley.
12. Serve the Hungarian goulash with barley hot, and enjoy the hearty and comforting flavors of this classic dish!

This Hungarian goulash with barley is perfect for a cozy dinner on a cold day, and it's sure to become a family favorite.

**Czech potato dumplings with sauerkraut**

Ingredients:

For the Potato Dumplings:

- 4 large potatoes, peeled and boiled until tender
- 1 cup all-purpose flour
- 1 egg
- 1 teaspoon salt

For the Sauerkraut:

- 1 lb (450g) sauerkraut, drained and rinsed
- 1 onion, finely chopped
- 2 tablespoons vegetable oil
- 1 teaspoon caraway seeds (optional)
- Salt and pepper to taste

Instructions:

1. Once the potatoes are boiled and tender, mash them thoroughly in a large mixing bowl.
2. Add the flour, egg, and salt to the mashed potatoes. Mix until well combined and a dough forms. If the dough is too sticky, you can add more flour as needed.
3. Bring a large pot of salted water to a boil.
4. While the water is heating, shape the potato dough into small dumplings. You can form them into balls or elongated shapes, whichever you prefer.
5. Carefully drop the dumplings into the boiling water, a few at a time, making sure not to overcrowd the pot. Cook for about 10-15 minutes, or until the dumplings float to the surface and are cooked through.
6. Once cooked, remove the dumplings from the water with a slotted spoon and set them aside.
7. In a large skillet, heat the vegetable oil over medium heat. Add the chopped onion and sauté until softened and translucent.

8. Add the drained and rinsed sauerkraut to the skillet, along with the caraway seeds if using. Cook for about 10-15 minutes, stirring occasionally, until the sauerkraut is heated through and tender.
9. Season the sauerkraut with salt and pepper to taste.
10. Serve the Czech potato dumplings with the sauerkraut hot, as a delicious and comforting meal.

Enjoy the flavors of this traditional Czech dish, perfect for a hearty dinner on a cold evening!

## Norwegian lefse (potato flatbread)

Ingredients:

- 4 cups riced or mashed potatoes (about 2 pounds)
- 1/2 cup unsalted butter, softened
- 1/4 cup heavy cream
- 1 teaspoon salt
- 1 1/2 cups all-purpose flour, plus more for rolling

Instructions:

1. Start by preparing the potatoes. You can either rice or mash the potatoes until smooth. Let them cool slightly before proceeding.
2. In a large mixing bowl, combine the mashed potatoes, softened butter, heavy cream, and salt. Mix until well combined.
3. Gradually add the all-purpose flour to the potato mixture, stirring until a soft dough forms. You may not need to use all of the flour, so add it gradually until the dough reaches the right consistency. The dough should be soft and slightly sticky but manageable.
4. Divide the dough into smaller portions and shape each portion into a ball. Cover the dough balls with a clean kitchen towel and let them rest for about 30 minutes.
5. Preheat a lefse griddle or a large skillet over medium heat. If you don't have a lefse griddle, a regular skillet will work fine.
6. On a lightly floured surface, roll out one dough ball at a time into a thin circle, about 1/8 inch thick. Use a rolling pin to achieve the desired thickness, and keep the surface and rolling pin lightly floured to prevent sticking.
7. Carefully transfer the rolled-out dough to the preheated griddle or skillet. Cook for about 1-2 minutes on each side, or until lightly golden brown and cooked through. Use a spatula to flip the lefse halfway through cooking.
8. Remove the cooked lefse from the griddle or skillet and transfer it to a clean kitchen towel. Cover with another towel to keep it warm while you cook the remaining dough.
9. Repeat the rolling and cooking process with the remaining dough balls until all the lefse are cooked.

10. Serve the Norwegian lefse warm, either plain or with your favorite toppings such as butter, sugar, cinnamon, or jam.

Enjoy the delicious taste and texture of homemade Norwegian lefse, perfect for any occasion or as a special treat during the holidays!

**Brazilian tapioca crepes with coconut filling**

Ingredients:

For the Tapioca Crepes:

- 1 cup tapioca flour (also known as tapioca starch)
- Pinch of salt
- Water, as needed

For the Coconut Filling:

- 1 cup shredded unsweetened coconut
- 1/2 cup sweetened condensed milk
- 2 tablespoons coconut milk or water
- Pinch of salt (optional)

Instructions:

1. Start by making the coconut filling. In a small saucepan, combine the shredded coconut, sweetened condensed milk, coconut milk or water, and a pinch of salt if desired. Cook over low heat, stirring constantly, until the mixture thickens slightly and the coconut is well coated with the milk, about 5-7 minutes. Remove from heat and set aside to cool.
2. While the coconut filling is cooling, make the tapioca crepes. In a mixing bowl, combine the tapioca flour and a pinch of salt. Gradually add water, stirring continuously, until a smooth and pliable dough forms. The dough should hold together well but not be too sticky.
3. Divide the dough into small balls, about the size of a golf ball.
4. Heat a non-stick skillet or crepe pan over medium heat. Place one dough ball in the center of the skillet and use your fingers to press and flatten it into a thin, round crepe, about 6-7 inches in diameter.
5. Cook the crepe for about 1-2 minutes on each side, or until lightly golden brown and cooked through. Use a spatula to flip the crepe halfway through cooking.

6. Remove the cooked crepe from the skillet and transfer it to a plate. Repeat the process with the remaining dough balls until all the crepes are cooked.
7. To assemble the tapioca crepes, spoon a portion of the coconut filling onto one half of each crepe. Fold the other half of the crepe over the filling to form a half-moon shape.
8. Serve the Brazilian tapioca crepes with coconut filling warm, and enjoy their delicious flavor and texture!

These tapioca crepes with coconut filling are a delightful and satisfying treat, perfect for breakfast, brunch, or any time you're craving a taste of Brazil!

www.ingramcontent.com/pod-product-compliance
Lightning Source LLC
LaVergne TN
LVHW061943070526
838199LV00060B/3947